THE CLASSIC AMERICAN QUILT COLLECTION®

◇

STARS

Written by Janet Wickell

Edited by Darra Duffy Williamson

 Rodale Press, Emmaus, Pennsylvania

OUR PURPOSE

*"We inspire and enable people to improve
their lives and the world around them."*

Library of Congress Cataloging-in-Publication Data

Wickell, Janet.
The classic American quilt collection. Stars / written
by Janet Wickell ; edited by Darra Duffy Williamson.
    p. cm.
   ISBN 0–87596–782–5 (alk. paper)
   1. Patchwork—United States—Patterns.
2. Quilting—United States—Patterns. 3. Patchwork
quilts—United States. 4. Stars in art. I. Williamson,
Darra Duffy. II. Title.
TT835.W52   1996
746.46'041—dc20   96–33623

Distributed in the book trade by St. Martin's Press

2 4 6 8 10 9 7 5 3 1 hardcover

STARS EDITORIAL AND DESIGN STAFF

Technical Writer: *Janet Wickell*

Editor: *Darra Duffy Williamson*

Coordinating Editors: *Suzanne Nelson,
Karen Bolesta, Karen Costello Soltys,
Sarah Dunn*

Cover and Interior Designer: *Denise M. Shade*

Book Layout: *Tanya L. Lipinski*

Design Assistance: *Karen Lomax, Jen Miller*

Photographer: *Mitch Mandel*

Illustrators: *Mario Ferro, Jackie Walsh*

Copy Editor: *Erana Bumbardatore*

Manufacturing Coordinator: *Patrick Smith*

Editorial Assistance: *Sue Nickol,
Jodi Rehl, Lori Schaffer*

RODALE HOME AND GARDEN BOOKS

Vice President and Editorial Director:
Margaret J. Lydic

Managing Editor: *Suzanne Nelson*

Art Director: *Paula Jaworski*

Associate Art Director: *Mary Ellen Fanelli*

Studio Manager: *Leslie Keefe*

Copy Director: *Dolores Plikaitis*

Production Manager: *Helen Clogston*

Office Manager: *Karen Earl-Braymer*

If you have any questions or comments concerning
the editorial content of this book, please write to:
   Rodale Press, Inc.
   Book Readers' Service
   33 East Minor Street
   Emmaus, PA 18098

The cover quilt is "My Stars! . . . They're Plaid!" and
can be found on page 2.

CONTENTS

Acknowledgments

My Stars!...They're Plaid!, made by Betty L. Alvarez of Marietta, Georgia. A quilter since 1978, Betty is the past president and quilt show chair of the East Cobb Quilter's Guild. Making this quilt helped her explore designing quilts with "movement." In 1991 and 1992, it won awards at several shows and was featured in *Quilt World* magazine.

Swing on a Star, made by Sharyn Craig of El Cajon, California. Sharyn is a quiltmaker and teacher who usually makes colorful scrap quilts and admits that making this basically two-color quilt took real willpower. This quilt is one of several made by Sharyn that combines the Swing in the Center and Indian Hatchet blocks in different arrangements.

Reflections, made by Patricia Mahoney of Santa Maria, California. A quilter for 30 years, Patricia pieced this quilt by both hand and machine, working on much of it during her husband's illness. This quilt won honors at three quilt shows in 1991, including the California State Fair, and was also published in *Award-Winning Quilts and Their Makers* in 1991. Patricia is a member of the Santa Maria Valley Quilt Guild.

Broken Star, made by Kathryn E. Larson England of Lewiston, Idaho. Kathryn first tried quilting in 1980, when her husband started medical school, and she's been "hooked" ever since. She made this quilt as a gift for her husband. It appeared in the Summer 1993 issue of *Old Fashioned Patchwork*. Kathryn is a member of the Seaport Quilters Guild in Lewiston.

Feathered World without End, made by Valerie Schadt of Fayetteville, New York. A quilter for 15 years, Valerie designed and hand quilted the patterns on this quilt, which won an honorable mention in 1995 at the Pennsylvania National Quilting Extravaganza in Fort Washington, Pennsylvania. It was also displayed at Quilting by the Lake in Morrisville, New York. Valerie is active in her local quilt guild as well as in a more modern version, Genie On-line Quilters.

Trailing Starflower, made by Bethany S. Reynolds of Ellsworth, Maine. Bethany, a quilter for 13 years, teaches quilting throughout New England and runs a pattern publishing business from her home. She belongs to the Pine Tree Quilters Guild (the Maine state guild) and the New England Quilters Guild.

Sister's Choice, owned by Angela Dominy of Livingston, Texas. The blocks for this quilt were made by members of the Kingwood Area Quilt Guild. It was designed and assembled by Bev Rogers and machine quilted by Dori Hawks. The block was chosen to celebrate the sisterhood among quilters everywhere. The quilt won second place for group quilts in Houston in 1994, and it appeared in the April 1995 issue of *Quilter's Newsletter Magazine*. Angela won the quilt in a raffle.

Origami Stars, made by Doris Krauss Adomsky of Ivyland, Pennsylvania. A quiltmaker and teacher, Doris admits her favorite part of quilting is achieving precise points. She is a member of the Newtown Quilters Guild, and she designed and made this quilt in just two weeks as a sample for a class.

Feathered Star, owned by Kathlyn F. Sullivan of Raleigh, North Carolina. Kathlyn bought this quilt from an antique dealer, who dates it from 1915. It was made in Surry County, North Carolina.

Solitude, made by Johanna Wilson of Walnut Grove, Minnesota, and machine quilted by Bonnie Erickson. Johanna has been quilting since 1984, and right from the start she began to think of design variations. Her pattern business, Plum Creek Patchwork, has over 25 patterns available, as well as *Bear Tracks in the Berry Patch,* a book of patterns.

Midnight in Paradise, made by Susan Stein of St. Paul, Minnesota. Susan is a quiltmaker (for 20 years!), quilt shop owner, teacher, and frequent contributor to quilt books and magazines. This quilt was made as a sample for her store and took only a few days to complete. Susan and her husband share their home with 100 quilts.

INTRODUCTION

To man, that was in th'evening made,
stars gave the first delight;
Admiring, in the gloomy shade,
Those little drops of light.
(Edmund Waller—*An Apology for Having Looked Before*)

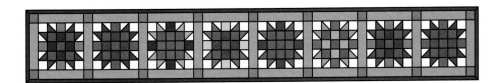

Stars and quilts are a heavenly combination, one that was surely born not long after women first began stitching bits of colored fabrics together. Quilt historians have discovered star patterns among some of the earliest quilts, and there are those who believe that star blocks are among the few patterns that came from England in the late 1700s to take root as American quiltmaking grew into its own. Now, 200 years later, a walk through any of today's quilt shows reveals that the appeal of star quilts hasn't dimmed in the least.

Gaze up at the star-studded sky on a clear night and you'll get some sense of the astounding array of star quilt designs that is available to quiltmakers. Well over 100 distinct Star block patterns have been documented, and when you consider the variations that result from color and value placement, the creative possibilities are limitless. This smorgasbord of starry delights is a feast for quiltmakers—but a dilemma for quilt book editors. Amid all the possibilities, how would we ever narrow the selection down to the 11 that could fit between the covers of this book?

As we began our star search, we knew there were a couple of basic "must haves," like a Feathered Star and a Lone Star. Long considered to be the true test of expert piecing skills, we've updated the techniques needed for these patterns to take advantage

of the ease and accuracy of rotary cutting and quick piecing. We also knew that no book on Star quilts could be complete without the old standby, Variable Star. We provide two variations on this theme; one a handsome classic (Reflections, page 24), the other a zingy twist on tradition featuring bold and tropical fabrics (Midnight in Paradise, page 98). In our ongoing quest for the best, we also discovered how much innovative techniques like paper foundation piecing and three-dimensional fabric folds can enhance time-honored star quilts (check out Feathered World without End, page 42, and Origami Stars, page 76). We scoured the countryside for an appealing eight-pointed star and didn't stop until we found a winner. Trailing Starflower (page 56) gives you a chance to piece, appliqué, and even make decorative yo-yo accents!

Every single quilt in this book represents the best of both worlds—an appealing star design, plus directions that give you the easiest and most efficient way to put together a beautiful quilt. Each project is so unique and irresistible you may soon find yourself sewing up your own galaxy of twinkling stars—which is entirely fitting, because in quiltmaking, the sky's the limit!

Suzanne Nelson

Suzanne Nelson

STARS
PROJECTS

MY STARS!...THEY'RE PLAID!

Skill Level: *Easy*

Betty Alvarez of Marietta, Georgia, whipped up this extravaganza in plaid after being inspired by noted quiltmaker and fabric designer Roberta Horton. Betty's merry mix of madras plaids in vibrant hues makes this star quilt simply twinkle. A randomly pieced border adds a playful final touch—and it's a great way to use up the leftovers from a multi-fabric project.

BEFORE YOU BEGIN

This quilt is a combination of Garden Walk (similar to the traditional 54-40 or Fight block) and Four-in-Nine Patch blocks. Both blocks include 3-inch-square four patch blocks. Quick strip-piecing techniques make it easy to assemble the large quantity of four patches needed. See "Cutting Fabric" on page 115 for general information on rotary cutting.

The light-color triangles for the large and small star backgrounds are cut with templates made from pattern pieces A and B on page 10. When marking fabric, be sure the grain line drawn on the pattern is parallel to the fabric's straight of grain. For more information on making templates, see "Making and Using Templates" on page 116.

CHOOSING FABRICS

This scrap quilt was assembled with a large assortment of colorful woven and madras plaids. To make a quilt similar to the one shown, select as many different fabrics as possible. Like units within each block are identical, but the star blocks each contain three different units (four patches, large star points, and small star points), so each block requires three different plaid fabrics. Try to choose plaids of varying scale, and don't worry too much about color unless you would like to focus on a specific range. Notice in the quilt photograph on the opposite page that darker plaids are used in the outer areas of the quilt, with lighter values placed in blocks near the center. Muslin is used for the background throughout.

Fat quarters are a good choice for this quilt because they are wide and long enough to make several strip sets needed for the four patch units. Fat eighths are also suitable if their longest edge measures 22 inches. Star points can be cut from either fat quarters or fat eighths.

Quilt Sizes		
	Twin	Queen (shown)
Finished Quilt Size	73" × 91"	91" × 109"
Number of Star Blocks	32	50
Number of Alternate Blocks	31	49
Number of Four Patch Units	283	445

Materials		
Fabric	Twin	Queen
Assorted plaids	5½ yards	7 yards
Muslin	5¼ yards	8¼ yards
Backing	5⅝ yards	8⅓ yards
Batting	80" × 98"	98" × 116"
Binding	⅝ yard	⅔ yard

NOTE: *Yardages are based on 44/45-inch-wide fabrics that are at least 42 inches wide after preshrinking.*

Cutting Chart

Fabric	Used For	Strip Width or Piece	Number to Cut Twin	Number to Cut Queen	Second Cut Dimensions	Number to Cut Twin	Number to Cut Queen
Plaids	Four patches	2"	32	50	2" × 21"	63	99
	Large star points	2⅜"	15	23	2⅜" × 4¼"*	128	200
	Small star points	1¼"	8	12	1¼" × 2¼"*	128	200
	Small star centers	1½"	2	2	1½" squares	32	50
	Borders†	2" strips	—	—			
Muslin	Four patches	2"	32	50	2" × 21"	63	99
	Large star background	Template A	128	200			
	Small star background	Template B	128	200			
	Small star corners	1½"	5	8	1½" squares	128	200
	Alternate blocks	3½"	12	18	3½" squares	124	196

* *Cut four identical rectangles for each block.*

† *See Steps 1 and 2 in "Adding the Borders" on page 7.*

The Materials list suggests the total plaid yardage required to make this quilt, but as for most scrappy quilts, it may be helpful to think of yardage in terms of the total number of blocks and how many times you plan to repeat a fabric, instead.

To develop a unique color scheme for the quilt, photocopy the **Color Plan** on page 11, and use crayons or colored pencils to test different color arrangements.

CUTTING

All the rotary cutting dimensions and pattern pieces given for this quilt include ¼-inch seam allowances. Cut the number of strips and pieces as described in the Cutting Chart, then follow the directions below for additional cutting information. All strips are cut on the crosswise grain of the fabric.

Note: We recommend that you cut and piece a sample block before cutting all the fabric for your quilt.

For the star points, you will need to make mirror-image triangles. Cut half of the 2⅜ × 4¼-inch plaid rectangles for large star points in half diagonally from the top left to the bottom right, as shown in **Diagram 1A**. Cut the remaining rectangles in half diagonally in the opposite direction, from top right to bottom left, as shown in **1B**. Keep the triangles that you cut from the same fabric paired together.

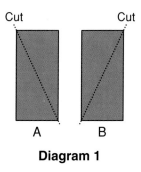

Diagram 1

Repeat the diagonal cutting for the 1¼ × 2¼-inch plaid rectangles for the small star blocks, cutting half in each direction, as shown in the above diagram. Keep the triangles that you cut from the same fabric paired together. For easy assembly of your block later, place a matching 1½-inch square with each set of eight triangles cut from the same plaid fabric.

PIECING THE LARGE STAR BLOCKS

Four Patch Units

A four patch unit is sewn into each corner of the Star block and at the corners and center of the Alternate block, as shown in the **Block Diagram.** The four patch units within individual blocks are identical, and can be made easily and accurately using a quick-piecing method.

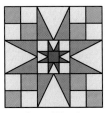 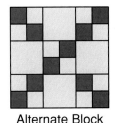

Star Block   Alternate Block

Block Diagram

Step 1. To make the four patch units for the Star blocks, sew a 2 × 21-inch plaid strip to a 2 × 21-inch muslin strip, as shown in **Diagram 2.** Press the seam allowance toward the plaid strip.

2"

Diagram 2

Step 2. Use your rotary cutting equipment to square up one end of the strip, and cut 2-inch segments from it, as shown in **Diagram 2.**

Step 3. Carefully match the center seams, and sew two segments together, as shown in **Diagram 3.** Press the seam in either direction. Sew the remaining segments together in pairs to make a total of four identical four patch units. Stack together.

Diagram 3

Step 4. Repeat Steps 1 through 3 to assemble the total number of four patch units required for

— Sew Easy —

When you cut pieces for a quilt block using rotary cutting *and* templates, as in this project, you may notice a variation in the size and fit of your pieces.

Tracing around a template can allow the shape to "grow" due to the width of the pencil line, which can be compounded by cutting along the outside of the drawn line. When you rotary cut, your cutter is positioned snugly against a ruler, which is aligned with the edge of the fabric at a precise measurement. No pencil lines are used.

Don't let the possibility of variation discourage you. It's a situation that can easily be avoided by doing the following things:

• Check your templates for accuracy.

• Use a very narrow pencil line to mark the fabric.

• Be sure to cut all template pieces at the innermost edge of the drawn line.

• As you cut, make sure the pieces match the patterns printed in the book.

• Piece a sample block to make sure all units match correctly. After a while, you will know exactly where to cut to produce accurate results.

your quilt size. Keep each identical set separate from the others if you plan to use like units within each block, as in the quilt shown on page 2.

Star Points

For each Star block, you'll need eight large triangles cut from identical plaid rectangles, four cut along one diagonal, four cut along the opposite diagonal, as shown in **Diagram 1** on the opposite page. While the triangles are cut from the same fabric, it should be a different fabric than you used in the four patch units.

Step 1. Use **Trimming Pattern 1** to trim points, as described in Sew Easy, below. Sew a pair of mirror image plaid triangles to either side of a muslin A triangle, as shown in **Diagram 4**. Press the seams toward the plaid triangles.

Diagram 4

Step 2. Repeat, assembling a total of four star point units for each large Star block in your quilt.

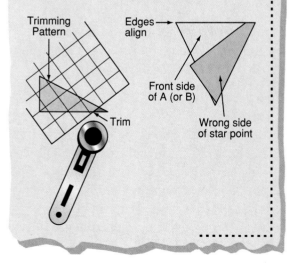

— Sew Easy

To align your triangles for stitching, trim the tips off the plaid triangles. Since these triangles are not cut at 45 degree angles, the alignment can be a little tricky. Make a paper template of **Trimming Pattern 1** on page 10. Tape it to the underside of a rotary ruler so the trimmed-off tip is flush with the straight edge of the ruler. Align your ruler over the star point triangles, and trim away the excess seam allowance from the triangle's tip with your rotary cutter. You can trim several triangles at a time if you have them carefully layered. **Trimming Pattern 2** is provided for the small star blocks that make up the centers of the large stars.

Trimming Pattern

Edges align →

Front side of A (or B)

Trim

Wrong side of star point

Small Star Block

Step 1. Assemble the small Star points in the same manner as you did the large ones. Use plaid triangles cut from the $1\frac{1}{4} \times 2\frac{1}{4}$-inch rectangles. Use **Trimming Pattern 2** to trim the plaid triangle points, as described in Sew Easy on this page, and attach them to the muslin B triangles.

Step 2. Lay out the components of the block: four star points units, a matching $1\frac{1}{2}$-inch plaid square, and four $1\frac{1}{2}$-inch muslin squares. Sew the pieces together in rows, as shown in **Diagram 5A**. Press the seam allowances in adjoining rows in opposite directions, then sew the rows together, as shown in **5B**. Press the block.

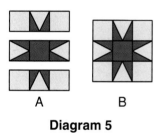

A   B

Diagram 5

Step 3. Repeat Steps 1 and 2 to make the number of small Star blocks for your quilt size.

— Sew Easy

If you prefer not to work with such small pieces, you can replace the 3-inch Star block with either a $3\frac{1}{2}$-inch (cut size) plaid square or an additional four patch unit made of leftovers from your plaid and muslin strip sets.

ASSEMBLING THE BLOCK

Step 1. Sew the four patch units, star points, and small Star block together in three rows, as shown in **Diagram 6A** on the opposite page. Press the seam allowances toward the large star points, then sew the rows together, as shown in **6B**. Press the block.

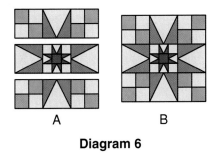

Diagram 6

Step 2. Repeat to complete the total number of large Star blocks required for your quilt size.

PIECING THE ALTERNATE BLOCKS

Step 1. Piece and lay out five identical four patch units and four 3½-inch muslin squares for the block, as shown in **Diagram 7A,** and sew the pieces into three rows. Note that the diagonal line from the lower left corner to the upper right corner is filled with dark patches. This same color layout is used for every Alternate block. Press seams in adjoining rows in opposite directions, then sew the rows together, as shown in **7B.** Press.

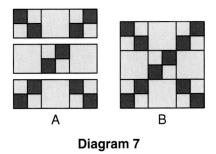

Diagram 7

Step 2. Repeat to make the total number of Alternate blocks required for your quilt size.

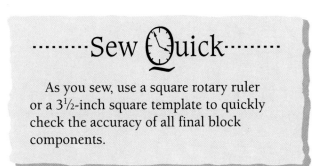

········Sew Quick········

As you sew, use a square rotary ruler or a 3½-inch square template to quickly check the accuracy of all final block components.

ASSEMBLING THE QUILT TOP

Step 1. Arrange the Star and Alternate blocks, as shown in the **Quilt Diagram** on page 9. The heavy line indicates the layout for the twin-size quilt. The queen-size quilt uses 99 blocks. Take care to orient all Alternate blocks as shown in the diagram so you achieve the desired diagonal effect. Rearrange the blocks until the color layout pleases you. Note that in the quilt shown on page 2, darker plaid blocks were placed around the perimeter of the quilt.

Step 2. Sew the blocks in each row together. When possible, press seams in adjoining rows in opposite directions. Sew the rows together, taking care to match all unit intersections. Press the quilt.

ADDING THE BORDERS

The quilt shown has three plaid scrap borders that each finish at 1½ inches wide, giving you a total finished border unit width of 4½ inches. The borders are made by sewing random lengths of plaid scraps end to end with angled seams. The border corners are mitered.

Step 1. To determine the length needed for the borders, measure the quilt top vertically through the center. To this measurement, add two times the finished width of the border unit plus 5 inches (4½ inches × 2 = 9 inches; 9 inches + 5 inches = 14 inches). This is the length you will need to make each of the side borders. Use the same method to calculate strip lengths needed for the top and bottom borders, measuring horizontally through the middle of the quilt.

Step 2. Cut 2-inch-wide strips from all of your plaid scraps. Don't worry if some of your scrap strips are longer than others. Most of the segments in the quilt shown here are approximately 6 to 24 inches long. In fact, if most of your strips are close to the same length, you may want to trim some of them so they are shorter, or cut some in half to make two shorter strips that can be used in different sections of your borders.

Step 3. Stack several strips together, right sides up with left ends aligned, as shown in **Diagram 8A.** Use your rotary ruler to cut a 45 degree angle at the left end of the stack, as shown in **8B.** Align the right ends and make another 45 degree cut through all layers, as shown in **8C.** Cuts should be parallel to each other. Cut approximately half of the 2-inch-wide strips in this fashion. Label them "Right and bottom border strips," and set them aside.

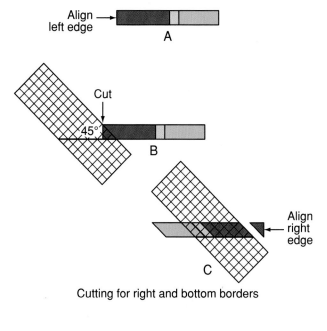

Cutting for right and bottom borders

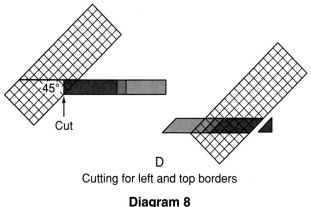

Cutting for left and top borders

Diagram 8

Step 4. For the remaining strips, reverse the cutting angle at each end, as shown in **8D.** Label these "Left and top border strips."

Step 5. Sew random-length right border and bottom border strips together end-to-end, as shown in **Diagram 9A,** until you achieve the required length calculated for one of these borders. Repeat, making a total of three border units for the right border and three for the bottom border.

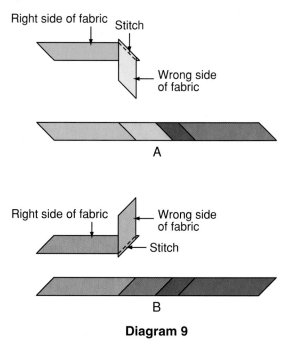

Diagram 9

Step 6. Repeat the process described in Step 5 with the random-length left and top border strips, as shown in **Diagram 9B,** to make three pieced border units for the left border and three for the top border.

Step 7. Working with the right side border units, pin and sew the three units together length-wise into a new larger unit, making sure the diagonal seams run in the same direction, as shown in **Diagram 10A.** Press the seams toward what will be the inner border. In the same manner, sew the three bottom border units into a single larger unit, pressing the seams toward the outer border.

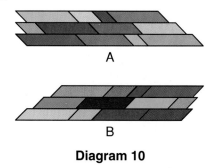

Diagram 10

Step 8. Repeat the process described in Step 7 with the appropriate strips to make the left side and top border units, as shown in **Diagram 10B.**

Step 9. Pin and sew the four border units to the appropriate sides of the quilt top, with the diag-onal seams oriented as shown in the **Quilt Diagram**. Refer to "Mitering Borders" on page 119 for instructions on adding borders with mitered corners. When preparing the miters, be sure to match seams in adjacent borders, as shown in the **Quilt Diagram.**

Quilt Diagram

QUILTING AND FINISHING

Step 1. Mark the top for quilting. Diagonal lines running through the dark squares in the four patches in both Star and Alternate blocks make an easy and effective quilting design. Extend these lines into the border. Quilting ¼ inch from seams in the star blocks can be "eyeballed" to save time marking.

Step 2. Regardless of which quilt size you've chosen to make, the backing will have to be pieced, as shown in **Diagram 11.** For the twin-size quilt, cut the backing fabric in half and trim the selvages. Cut one piece in half lengthwise, and sew a narrow panel to each side of the full-width piece. Press the seams open.

For the queen-size quilt, cut the backing fabric into three equal segments and trim the selvages. Cut a 38-inch-wide panel from two of the segments, and sew them to each side of the full-width piece. Press the seams open.

Step 3. Layer the backing, batting, and quilt top, and baste the layers together. Hand or machine quilt as desired.

Step 4. Referring to the directions on page 121, make and attach double-fold binding. The binding in the quilt shown finishes at a width of ½ inch. To make binding that finishes this wide, cut your binding strips 2½ inches wide. To calculate the total amount of binding you will need, add up the length of the four sides of the quilt, plus 9 inches.

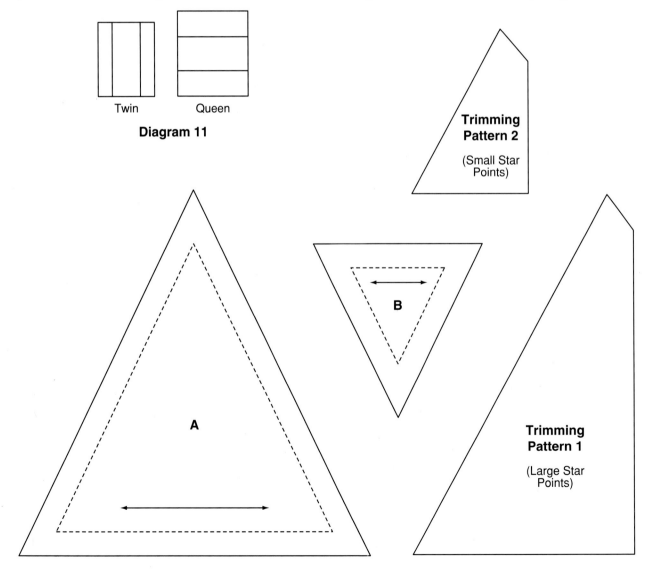

Twin   Queen

Diagram 11

Trimming Pattern 2

(Small Star Points)

B

A

Trimming Pattern 1

(Large Star Points)

My Stars!...They're Plaid!

Color Plan

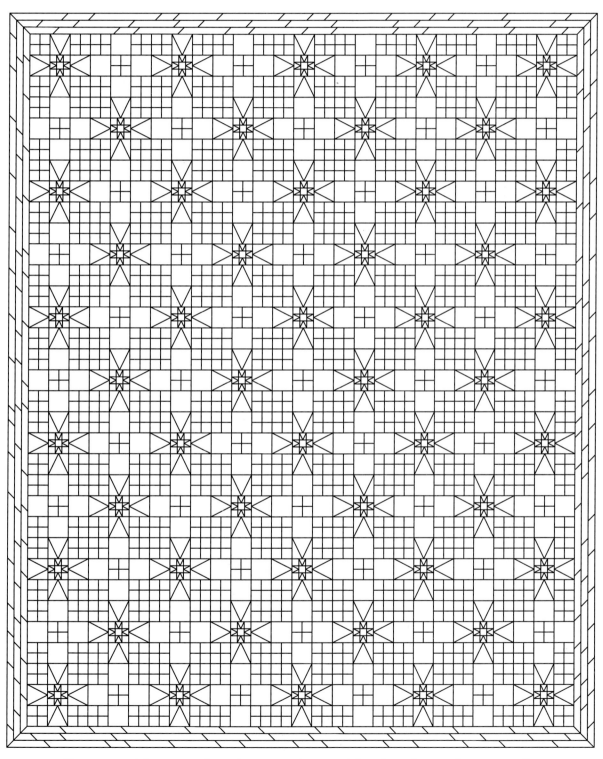

Photocopy this page and use it to experiment with color schemes for your quilt.

SWING ON A STAR

Skill Level: *Intermediate*

*S*haryn Craig, quiltmaker, teacher, and columnist, is noted for trying to get her students to think about new possibilities in their quiltmaking by asking, "What if…?" Swing on a Star is Sharyn's own answer to: "What if you start with a Garden Maze setting, add a few triangles to create a star motif, set the whole thing together with sashing strips, and use only black, white, and gray?" The answer is a striking, high-contrast quilt with lots of interest and movement.

BEFORE YOU BEGIN

This intricate-looking design features stars set on-point, separated by sashing strips and squares. Alternate blocks surround the stars and extend into the outer border. Finally, inverted prairie points are placed around the outer edges of the quilt, then appliquéd in place to complete the design.

Looks can be deceiving, however, as the construction of this quilt is not nearly as complex as the finished quilt would have you believe. With the exception of a few simple shapes that require templates, all of the pieces are strips, squares, and triangles that are rotary cut. Since all of the Star blocks are identical, a simple chain-piecing method makes assembly easy and efficient. Refer to "Stars Basics" on page 104, and "Cutting Fabric" on page 115 for information on rotary-cutting and chain-piecing techniques.

CHOOSING FABRICS

To make a quilt similar to the one shown, choose fabrics ranging from light gray to black.

Quilt Size	
Finished Quilt Size	42½" × 57¼"
Finished Block Size	9"
Number of Star Blocks	8
Number of Alternate Blocks	6

NOTE: *Due to the complexity of the quilt design, no size variations are provided.*

Materials	
Fabric	Amount
Medium gray floral print	1⅝ yards
Medium gray subtle print	1 yard
Black-and-gray print	⅞ yard
Black subtle print	⅝ yard
Medium light gray subtle print	⅜ yard
Light gray subtle print	10" square
Backing	2⅞ yards
Batting	50" × 65"
Binding	⅝ yard

NOTE: *Yardages are based on 44/45-inch-wide fabrics that are at least 42 inches wide after preshrinking.*

Some of the fabrics in this quilt appear to be solids, but in fact they are subtle, overall prints. All are slightly different in value, so when placed side by side, their contrast defines the individual pieces. The quilt contains a tone-on-tone, medium-scale floral print, used in the outer borders, and a larger, bold print in shades of black and gray that defines the Garden Path and inner border.

13

Cutting Chart

Fabric	Used For	Strip Width or Pieces	Number to Cut	Second Cut Dimensions	Number to Cut
Medium gray floral print*	M	Template M	2		
	J	3⅜"	1	3⅜" squares	5
	N	5¾"	4	5¾" × 28"	8
Medium gray subtle print	C	2⅜"	2	2⅜" squares	32
	B	4¼"	1	4¼" squares	8
	E	2⅝"	1	2⅝" squares	8
	G	8⅜"	2	8⅜" squares	6
Black-and-gray print	D	2⅝"	5	Template D	32
	F	2⅝"	2	Template F	6
	I	2"	1	2" squares	17
	K, K(r)	2⅝"	2	Template K	4
				Template K(r)	4
Black print	A, A(r)	2"	4	Template A	32
				Template A(r)	32
	O	4⅞"	2	4⅞" squares	13
	P	4⅜" squares	2		
Medium light gray print	H	2"	6	2" × 9½"	24
Light gray print	L	4⅞" squares	2		

* For best use of fabric, cut these pieces along the lengthwise grain.

The black and gray color scheme is elegant and contemporary, but this design would be equally effective in Christmas red and green, cozy red and blue homespuns, or any other high-contrast color scheme you like.

To develop your own color scheme, photocopy the **Color Plan** on page 23, and use crayons or colored pencils to experiment with different color arrangements.

CUTTING

The pieces for this quilt are cut using a combination of templates and rotary-cutting techniques. Make templates for pieces A, A(r), D, F, K, K(r), and M from the patterns on pages 21–22. (Flip a template to reverse it.) Refer to page 116 for complete instructions on making and using templates.

········ Sew Quick ········

When you are breaking down a pattern—or an entire quilt—to assign "names" to the pieces, letter them in the alphabetical order in which they will most logically be assembled. This easy "alphabet method" will help you to remember the piecing order no matter how many—or how long—the interruptions to your stitching time!

All rotary-cutting measurements and pattern pieces include ¼-inch seam allowances. Refer to the Cutting Chart for the number of pieces or strips to cut from each fabric. For easy reference, each piece is labeled by letter in the **Block Diagram** or **Assembly Diagram** on page 18. With the exception of the medium gray floral print (J, M, and N), cut all strips across the width of the fabric (crosswise grain).

Note: We recommend you cut and piece a sample block before cutting all of your fabric.

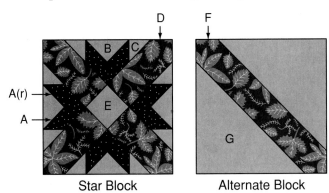

Block Diagram

Star Block · Alternate Block

After you have cut the strips and pieces, you will need to make the following sub-cuts:

• For the black A star points, layer two 2-inch-wide black strips with their right sides together, and use template A to cut the star point parallelograms, as shown in **Diagram 1**. By layering the strips, you will be cutting both A and A reverse pieces at the same time. Cut 32 each of A and A(r).

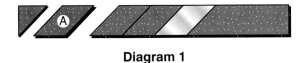

Diagram 1

• Cut the 4⅜-inch black squares in half diagonally, as shown in **Diagram 2A**, for the prairie point P triangles in the corners of the outer border.

• Cut the 4⅞-inch black squares in half twice diagonally, as shown in **Diagram 2B**. These prairie point O triangles point inward along the outer edges of the quilt.

• Cut the 4⅞-inch light gray squares in half diagonally, as shown in **Diagram 2A**. These will be used for the L corner triangles in the inner border.

• Cut the 3⅜-inch medium gray floral squares in half diagonally in both directions, as shown in **Diagram 2B**. These will be used for the J triangles in the inner border.

• To cut the black-and-gray print K and K reverse pieces, place two 2⅝-inch strips with their right sides together. Trace around the K template. By layering the strips, you will be cutting both K and K(r) pieces at the same time. Cut four each of K and K(r).

• Cut the 2⅜-inch medium gray subtle print squares in half diagonally (see **Diagram 2A**) for the Star block C background triangles.

• Cut the 4¼-inch medium gray subtle print squares in half diagonally in both directions (see **Diagram 2B**) for the Star block B background triangles.

• Cut the 8⅜-inch medium gray subtle print squares in half diagonally (see **Diagram 2A**) for the alternate block G triangles.

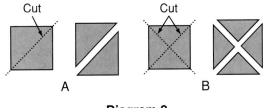

Cut · Cut

A · B

Diagram 2

PIECING THE STAR BLOCKS

Step 1. Place a black A and a black A reverse piece with right sides together. Sew them together, stopping ¼ inch from the edge, as indicated by the arrow in **Diagram 3**. Finger press the seam allowance toward the left star tip (when you have the right side of the fabric facing you, with the V-shape pointing down).

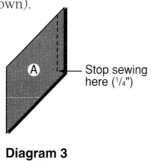

Diagram 3

Step 2. Position a medium gray B triangle as shown in **Diagram 4A**. Begin sewing ¼ inch from the tip of the B triangle at the point indicated by a dot in **4B**. Start with a backstitch, and sew outward in the direction indicated by each arrow. Refer to page 117 for details on working with set-in seams. Finger press seams toward the A pieces.

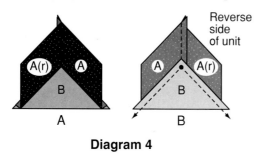

Diagram 4

Step 3. Sew a short side of a medium gray C triangle to each side of the star point unit, as shown in **Diagram 5**. Finger press seam allowances toward the C triangles. Label these Unit 1.

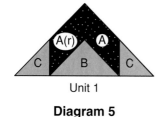

Diagram 5

Step 4. Repeat Steps 1 through 3 to make four Unit 1 segments for each block (a total of 32 for the entire quilt).

Step 5. Sew a Unit 1 segment to each side of a black-and-gray D piece, as shown in **Diagram 6**. Press all seam allowances toward D. Label these Unit 2. Repeat to assemble two Unit 2 segments for each of your blocks, to make a total of 16 Unit 2 segments for the entire quilt.

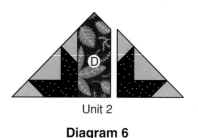

Unit 2

Diagram 6

Step 6. Sew D pieces to opposite sides of a medium gray E square, as shown in **Diagram 7**. Press seam allowances toward the D pieces. Label these Unit 3. Make a total of eight Unit 3 segments, one for each block.

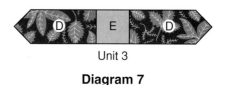

Unit 3

Diagram 7

Step 7. To complete each Star block, sew a Unit 2 from Step 5 to each long side of a Unit 3 from Step 6, as shown in **Diagram 8**. Make a total of eight blocks. Press the blocks carefully.

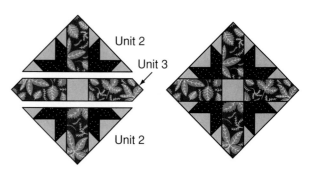

Diagram 8

MAKING THE ALTERNATE BLOCKS

Sew a medium gray G triangle to one long side of a black-and-gray print F piece, as shown in **Diagram 9**. Press seam allowances toward the triangle. Repeat, making a total of six alternate blocks. The remaining G triangle will be joined to the block when the outer border is attached to the quilt.

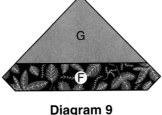

Diagram 9

ASSEMBLING THE CORNER UNITS

Step 1. Sew a medium gray floral J triangle to the left end of a black-and-gray K piece, as shown in **Diagram 10A**. Repeat, this time sewing a J triangle to the right end of a K reverse piece, as shown in **10B**. Make four each of these K and K(r) units. Press the seam allowances toward K.

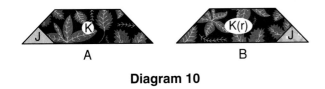

Diagram 10

Step 2. Place a K unit and a K reverse unit with right sides together. Sew them together, stopping ¼ inch from the edge, as indicated by the arrow in **Diagram 11**. Press to one side.

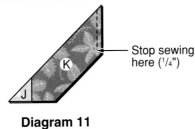

Diagram 11

Step 3. Position a light gray L corner triangle as shown in **Diagram 12A**. Begin sewing ¼ inch

from the right angle of the L triangle, at the point indicated by a dot in **12B**. Start with a backstitch, and sew outward in the direction indicated by each arrow. Press the seam allowances away from the L triangles. Repeat to make four of these corner units.

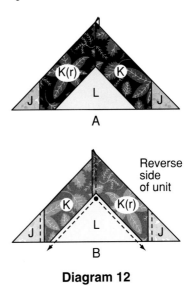

Diagram 12

ASSEMBLING THE QUILT TOP

Step 1. Use a design wall to arrange the Star blocks, the alternate blocks, the corner units, the H sashing strips, the I corner squares, and the remaining J sashing triangles into diagonal rows, as shown in the **Assembly Diagram** on page 18.

Step 2. Sew the blocks and sashing components together to form diagonal rows. When a gray J triangle is sewn to an alternate block, press toward the block.

Step 3. Sew the rows together, matching seam intersections carefully. Attach the corner units last. Press the seam allowances away from the sashing strips.

PIECING AND ADDING THE OUTER BORDER

Step 1. Sew a medium gray print G triangle to each side of an M piece, as shown in **Diagram 13** on page 18. Press the seams toward the M piece.

J

J I J   K(r)

H

L

H

← K

← J

Add corners last

Assembly Diagram

Repeat to make two of these border units, one each for the side borders.

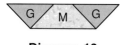

G   M   G

Diagram 13

Step 2. Layer two 5¾ × 28-inch medium gray floral print N border strips right sides together. Use your rotary cutter and ruler or the angled edge of template M to cut a 45 degree angle at the

left end of the layered strips, as shown in **Diagram 14.** Repeat to cut a total of four pairs of border strips. By layering the strips, you will have a pair of reverse-angled strips for each border.

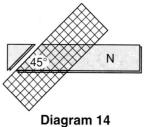

45°   N

Diagram 14

Step 3. Sew the appropriately angled edge of a trimmed N border strip to each end of a G-M-G border unit, as shown in **Diagram 15**. Press the seam allowances toward the N pieces. Make two of these border strips for each side border.

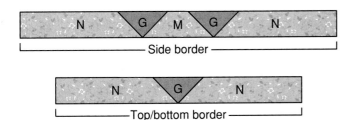

Diagram 15

Step 4. To make the top and bottom borders, sew the properly angled edges of a trimmed N border strip to the short sides of a medium gray floral G triangle, as shown in **Diagram 15**. Press the seams toward the N pieces.

Step 5. Pin and sew the top, bottom, and side borders to the quilt top, matching seams carefully where the medium gray G triangles meet the black and gray F strip to form the alternate blocks. Refer to page 119 in "Quiltmaking Basics" for detailed instructions on adding borders with mitered corners.

ADDING THE APPLIQUÉ PRAIRIE POINTS

The outer border of this quilt is finished with an inverted, appliqué prairie-point edge. Refer to page 109 for suggestions on preparing pieces for appliqué and for assistance with appliqué techniques. You will need to prepare all O and P prairie-point triangles for appliqué as instructed in the directions that follow.

Step 1. Use your preferred method to prepare the *longest* edge of each black P triangle by turning under a ¼-inch seam allowance, as shown in **Diagram 16A**. Then align and pin a black P triangle right side up to each corner of the quilt, as shown in **16B**.

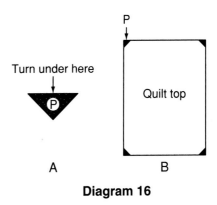

Diagram 16

Step 2. Use your preferred method to prepare the two *short* sides of each black O triangle by turning under a ¼-inch seam allowance, as shown in **Diagram 17**.

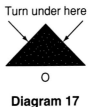

Diagram 17

Step 3. Place the quilt on a design wall or other flat surface. Position the triangles along the outer border around the perimeter of the quilt, overlapping as necessary for a balanced fit. Make sure that the triangles are pointed inward and that the longest edge of each O triangle is aligned with an outer edge of the quilt, as shown in the **Quilt Diagram** on page 20. Do not cover the tips of the medium gray G triangles. The quilt shown has fourteen O triangles along the top and bottom edges, and ten O triangles on each side border, but you will have a few extra "just in case." Pin or baste all triangles in place.

Step 4. Hand or machine stitch each O and P triangle to the quilt top, using your preferred method of appliqué.

QUILTING AND FINISHING

Step 1. Mark the quilt top for quilting. The quilt shown is machine quilted. The Star blocks are outline quilted, with the star design continued into the alternate blocks. Related geometric designs are used elsewhere in the quilt, and a series of diagonal lines are quilted in the borders.

Step 2. To make the quilt backing, cut the backing fabric in half crosswise and trim the selvages. Cut two 12-inch-wide panels from the entire length of one piece, then sew a narrow panel to each side of the full-width piece, as shown in **Diagram 18.** Press the seams open.

Diagram 18

Quilt Diagram

Step 3. Layer the quilt top, backing, and batting, and baste the layers together. Quilt by hand or machine, adding additional quilting as desired.

Step 4. Referring to the directions on page 121 in "Quiltmaking Basics," make and attach double-fold binding. To calculate the total amount of binding you will need, add up the length of the four sides of the quilt, then add an extra 9 inches. That number will give you the total approximate number of inches of double-fold binding you will need.

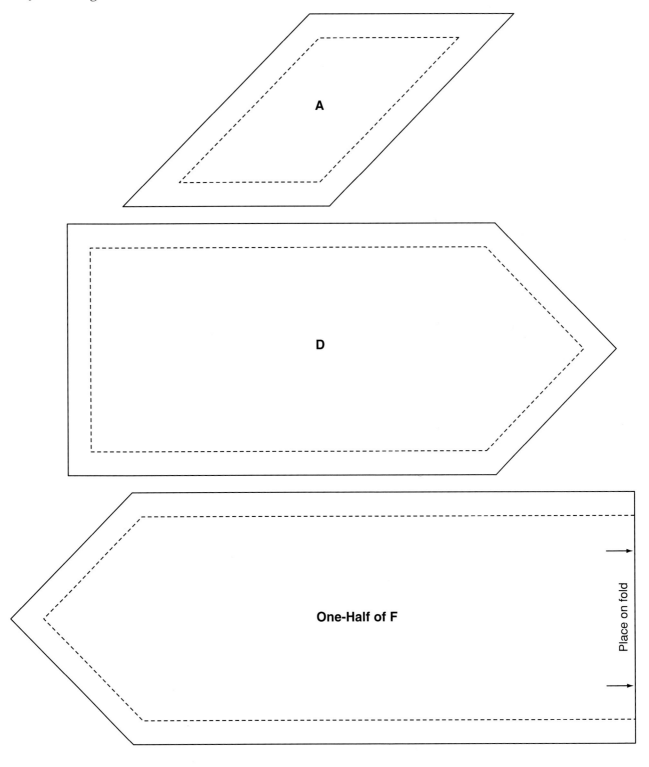

A

D

One-Half of F

Place on fold

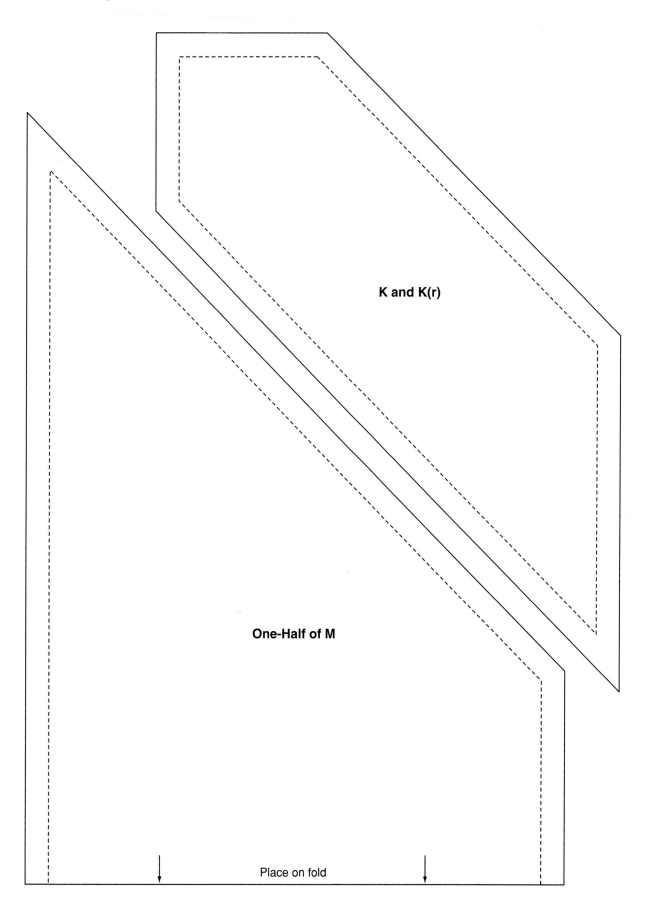

K and K(r)

One-Half of M

Place on fold

SWING ON A STAR

Color Plan

Photocopy this page and use it to experiment with color schemes for your quilt.

REFLECTIONS

Skill Level: *Intermediate*

If you love the rich, warm look of nineteenth-century scrap quilts, this elegant beauty will be irresistible. Patricia Mahoney of Santa Maria, California, has employed a treasure-trove of printed fabrics to lift this simple, time-honored pattern to celestial heights. A subtle variation in the choice of setting blocks and a sparkling pieced border helped earn this quilt a well-deserved prize at the 1991 American Quilter's Society Show in Paducah, Kentucky.

———————◆———————

BEFORE YOU BEGIN

Although the scrappy look of this quilt does not lend itself to many of the familiar quick-piecing methods, the directions include a variety of quick-cutting techniques that are sure to save you lots of time. Your fabrics can be layered for even more efficient cutting.

Read through "Stars Basics," beginning on page 104, and "Quiltmaking Basics," beginning on page 112, before you begin this quilt. You'll find lots of helpful hints and tips, in addition to specific instructions concerning the use of the rotary cutter.

CHOOSING FABRICS

Many of the colors and prints sewn into this scrappy quilt are reminiscent of fabrics from past eras, including reproductions of fabrics dating back to the mid- to late-1800s. At first glance, some fabrics in the quilt appear to be solid colors, but closer inspection reveals that they are all prints of varying scale, adding texture and visual interest to the piece. While

Quilt Sizes

	Double	Queen (shown)
Finished Quilt Size	83¼" × 94½"	94½" × 105¾"
Finished Star Block Size	8"	8"
Number of Star Blocks	35	48

Materials

Fabric	Double	Queen
Assorted light, medium, and dark scraps/prints (*total*)	3¼ yards	4¼ yards
Border stripe print*	2¾ yards	3⅛ yards
Medium-dark print	1¼ yards	2 yards
Medium print	1¼ yards	1¼ yards
Subtle wine print	1⅛ yards	1½ yards
Bright pink print†	—	fat ¼ yard
Light beige subtle print	⅜ yard	⅜ yard
Medium beige print	⅜ yard	⅝ yard
Backing	7¾ yards	8⅔ yards
Batting	91" × 102"	102" × 113"
Binding	⅝ yard	⅝ yard

NOTE: *Yardages are based on 44/45-inch-wide fabrics that are at least 42 inches wide after preshrinking.*

* *For single, continuous border strips. Assumes that both the inner narrow stripe border and the wide outer stripe border will be cut from the same striped fabric. Also assumes that the borders will be cut on the lengthwise grain and that there are four border repeats across the width of the fabric.*

† *Bright pink fabric is not required for the double-size quilt.*

Cutting Chart

Fabric	Used For	Strip Width or Pieces	Number to Cut Double	Number to Cut Queen	Second Cut Dimensions	Number to Cut Double	Number to Cut Queen
Assorted prints/scraps	H	2½" squares	108	124			
Wine print	Inner border*	1¼"	8	9			
	F	12½" squares	5	6			
	G	12⅜" squares	2	2			
Medium/ dark print	E (setting square 1)	8½"	5	8	8½" squares	18	29
Medium print	E (setting square 2)	8½"	5	5	8½" squares	18	18
Pink print	E (setting square 3)	8½"	—	1	8½" squares	—	2
Light beige print	I	4⅛"	3	3	4⅛" squares	26	30
Medium beige print	I	4⅛"	3	4	4⅛" squares	27	31
Border stripe	Inner border†	1"	4	4			
	Outer border†	4"	4	4			

* You may need to wait before cutting these strips because the width may vary. Refer to the instructions for "Adding the Double Inner Borders," Step 1, page 29.

† Strips cut on the lengthwise grain. Exact length of these strips will be determined after the quilt top has been assembled.

Cutting Chart for Individual Star Blocks

Fabric	Used For	Size to Cut	Number to Cut per Star Block
Assorted light, medium, and dark prints/scraps	A	2⅞" squares	4
	B	5¼" squares	1
	C	4½" squares	1
	D	2½" squares	4

NOTE: Cut all B and D pieces for each Star block from a single fabric, if possible. Cut A and C pieces from two different, contrasting fabrics.

many of the colors are subdued, the quiltmaker avoided a drab appearance by including a sprinkling of pinks, reds, golds, and other light, bright colors, much as her nineteenth-century predecessors might have done.

The placement of value within the Star blocks is varied. In some, dark stars stand out against a lighter background, while in others, the placement of lights and darks is reversed. A few Star blocks contain fabrics with very little difference in value. This mixture adds to the scrappy flavor of the quilt, as well as to its authentic, old-time appearance. To capture a similar look, plan to use *at least* 10 light, 20 dark, and 20 medium-value fabrics.

The quiltmaker used two different medium-scale prints for the setting squares, then tossed in two brighter pink setting squares for an extra spark of color in the center of the quilt. (These pink squares are eliminated in the double-size quilt because of the adjusted layout.)

The setting triangles and inner border are cut from a rich, subtle wine print fabric, which gives the blocks the appearance of floating against the background. A striped border print is used in the outer border and in the narrow strip sewn next to the pieced border.

The pieced border provides a great opportunity to use your scraps! You'll want to include as many different fabrics as you can to make this border twinkle against the darker surrounding borders. The pieced border is finished with triangles sewn from two prints, one slightly darker than the other, but both lighter than most of the colored squares in the border.

To develop your own color scheme, photocopy the **Color Plan** on page 33, and use crayons or colored pencils to experiment with different color arrangements.

CUTTING

All measurements include ¼-inch seam allowances. Refer to the Cutting Chart and cut the required number of pieces and strips in the sizes needed. Except for the border stripes, cut all strips across the fabric width (crosswise grain).

No templates are required for this project, since every piece is rotary cut. For easy reference, however, a letter identification for each pattern piece is given in the **Block Diagram** and in the **Queen-Size Assembly Diagram** on page 28.

You will need to cut some of the squares into triangles, as follows:

• For the star points (A triangles), cut the 2⅞-inch squares in half diagonally. Follow the same procedure to cut the two 12⅜-inch squares for the wine print corner triangles (piece G).

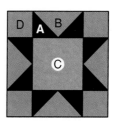

Block Diagram

• For the star background triangles (piece B), cut each of the 5¼-inch squares diagonally in *each* direction.

• For the wine print setting triangles (piece F), cut each of the 12½-inch squares diagonally in each direction.

• For the pieced border triangles (piece I), cut each of the 4⅛-inch squares diagonally in each direction.

Note: Cut and piece a sample block before cutting all the fabric for your quilt.

PIECING THE STAR BLOCKS

Each Star block consists of eight matching star points (A), a contrasting star center (C), and four each matching background triangles (B) and squares (D). The placement of lights and darks, as well as the actual fabrics, will vary from block to block. Refer to the **Block Diagram** and lay out each block before you begin to sew, experimenting until you find a color/value arrangement that pleases you and suits your fabrics. The quilt photograph on page 24, "Choosing Fabrics" on page 25, and page 106 of "Stars Basics" offer ideas and suggestions.

Step 1. Sew a star point A triangle to each short side of a background B triangle, as shown in **Diagram 1**. Press all the seam allowances toward the A triangles. Make four identical triangle units for each of your blocks.

Diagram 1

Step 2. Sew a triangle unit to the top and bottom edges of a contrasting C square, as shown in **Diagram 2**. Press the seams toward the center square.

Diagram 2

Step 3. Sew a background D square to each end of the remaining triangle units, as shown in **Diagram 3A**. Press the seams toward the squares. Sew one of these strips to each side of the block, as shown in **3B**. Press the seams as desired.

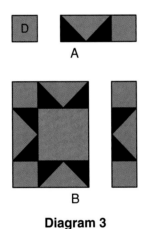

Diagram 3

·········Sew Quick·········

Maintain good pressing habits: Be sure to press all seam allowances as you go, pressing toward the darker fabric whenever possible. Use a dry iron, as steam may cause distortion. Be certain that the heat setting is appropriate for the fiber content. Remember that the key word is *press*; do not drag the iron back and forth across the pieces since this, too, can pull them out of shape.

Step 4. Repeat Steps 1 through 3 to make the total number of blocks required for your quilt.

ASSEMBLING THE QUILT TOP

Step 1. Use a design wall or other flat surface to arrange the Star blocks, setting squares (E), setting triangles (F), and corner triangles (G) into diagonal rows, as shown in the **Queen-Size Assembly Diagram**. (You will have a few F triangles left over.) Refer to the **Double-Size Quilt Diagram** on page 31 for assistance in laying out the double-size quilt. In each case, rearrange the Star blocks until you have achieved a balance of color and value that pleases you. The **Queen-Size Assembly Diagram** is color-coded to indicate the placement of each of the three different setting squares.

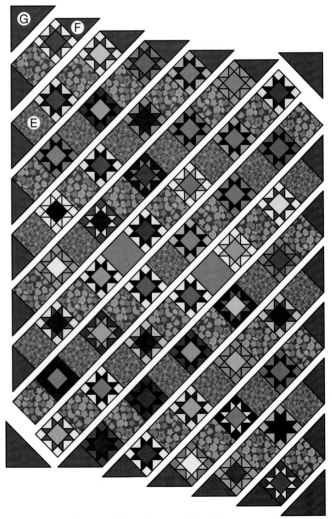

Queen-Size Assembly Diagram

Step 2. Sew the Star blocks, setting squares, and setting triangles together to form diagonal rows, as shown in the **Queen-Size Assembly Diagram**. Press seams toward the setting squares and triangles. Then sew the diagonal rows together, matching seam intersections carefully. Add the four corner triangles, and press the quilt.

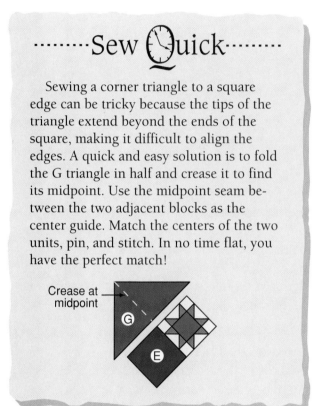

·········Sew Quick·········

Sewing a corner triangle to a square edge can be tricky because the tips of the triangle extend beyond the ends of the square, making it difficult to align the edges. A quick and easy solution is to fold the G triangle in half and crease it to find its midpoint. Use the midpoint seam between the two adjacent blocks as the center guide. Match the centers of the two units, pin, and stitch. In no time flat, you have the perfect match!

Crease at midpoint

ADDING THE BORDERS

The quilt shown has four mitered borders. The wine print and narrow stripe borders are sewn together and added as a single unit. The pieced border is constructed and added next. The wide stripe border is added last.

Adding the Double Inner Borders

Step 1. Check to be sure that your quilt top has been pressed thoroughly. Then measure through the quilt's horizontal and vertical centers to be certain that your quilt measures properly. Before the first border is added, the double-size quilt should measure about $68\frac{1}{2} \times 79\frac{3}{4}$ inches, including the seam allowances. The queen-size quilt should measure $79\frac{3}{4} \times 91$ inches, including the seam allowances. Slight variations are not unusual and can usually be accommodated by easing as the borders are added. If the dimensions of your quilt differ more substantially, adjust the *width* of the innermost (wine print) border to compensate for the difference, so that your pieced border will fit accurately. Refer to the Cutting Chart and cut the required number of wine print border strips for the quilt you are making, adjusting the width if necessary.

Step 2. To determine the correct *length* for the first two borders, begin with the vertical measurement of the quilt top determined in Step 1. To this measurement, add two times the finished width of the borders, plus 5 inches ($1\frac{1}{4}$ inches $\times$ 2 = $2\frac{1}{2}$ inches + 5 inches = $7\frac{1}{2}$ inches). This is the length you will need to make both the wine print and the narrow stripe strips for the two innermost side borders. Use the same method to calculate the length of the top and bottom borders, using the horizontal measurement determined in Step 1 as your base.

Step 3. Sew together wine print strips until you have achieved the length required for each border. (For the double-size quilt, each border will require two strips. For the queen-size quilt, the top and bottom borders will each require two strips, and each side border will require $2\frac{1}{2}$ strips.) Trim the strips to the exact length required and press.

Step 4. Cut each 1-inch-wide narrow stripe border in a single, continuous length as required for the side, the top, and the bottom border measurements. The 1-inch width includes the seam allowance.

Step 5. Beginning with the side border strips, pin and sew a wine print and a narrow stripe border strip together lengthwise to form a single side border unit. Press the seam toward the wine strip. Make two of these side border units. In the same manner, pin and sew the top and bottom border strips into units.

Step 6. Pin and sew the four border units to the appropriate sides of the quilt top, positioning the wine print border closest to the center of the quilt, as shown in the **Double-Size Quilt Diagram** on the opposite page. Match and pin the midpoints and attach the borders, stopping ¼ inch from the edge of the quilt, so that all four borders can be mitered later.

Assembling and Adding the Pieced Border

Step 1. Turn a 2½-inch H square on point, and sew a light I triangle to the top right edge and a medium I triangle to the lower left edge to make Unit 1, as shown in **Diagram 4**. Press the seam allowances toward the square, and label these Unit 1. Make the total number of Unit 1 segments required for your quilt size, as indicated in the Border Table. Note that the number of units needed is for *each* of the top, bottom, and side borders.

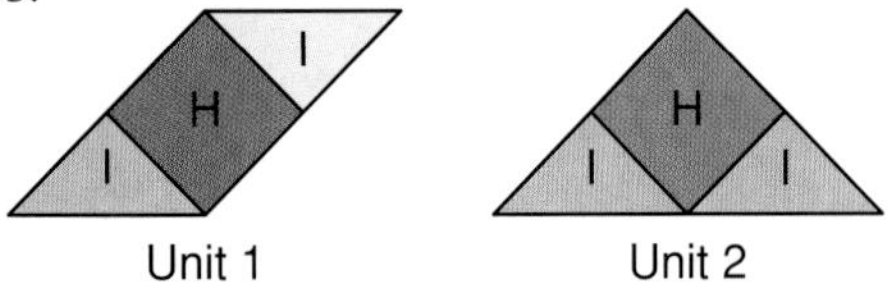

Unit 1   Unit 2

Diagram 4

Step 2. To make Unit 2, sew a medium I triangle to both the bottom left and the bottom right edges of the remaining four H squares, as shown in **Diagram 4**. Press the seam allowances toward the square, and label these Unit 2.

Border Table		
	Double	Queen
Total Unit 1	104	120
Total Unit 2	4	4
Top/Bottom Borders (*each*)	24 Unit 1	28 Unit 1
	1 Unit 2	1 Unit 2
Side Borders (*each*)	28 Unit 1	32 Unit 1
	1 Unit 2	1 Unit 2

Step 3. Refer to the Border Table. To assemble each pieced border, sew the required number of Unit 1 segments together along their diagonal edges, as shown in **Diagram 5A**. Finish the right edge of each border with a Unit 2 segment, as shown in **5B**, and press.

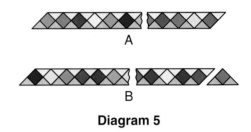

Diagram 5

Step 4. Sew the top, bottom, and side pieced borders to the appropriate sides of the quilt top, positioning the light I triangles closest to the center of the quilt, as shown in the **Quilt Diagrams**. For the best results, match the midpoint of each border to the midpoint of the corresponding edge of the quilt. Pin at the midpoints, and attach the borders, stopping ¼ inch from the edges of the quilt, so that the borders can be mitered after all four are attached.

Adding the Outer Border

Step 1. To determine the correct lengths for the outermost border, measure the quilt vertically and horizontally through its center, including the borders already added. Calculate the lengths of the strips, using the same method and formula as described in Step 2 of "Adding the Double Inner Borders."

Step 2. Cut each 4-inch-wide outer border from the border stripe in a single, continuous length as required for the side, the top, and the bottom border measurements.

Step 3. Sew each of the four borders to the appropriate edge of the quilt top. Match and pin the midpoints and follow the directions for adding mitered borders on page 119.

Step 4. Sew the mitered corners and press the seams open.

QUILTING AND FINISHING

Step 1. Mark the top for quilting. The Star blocks in the quilt shown were quilted in the ditch. Crosshatching of varying widths covers the rest of the quilt.

Step 2. The quilt backing will have to be pieced. **Diagram 6** illustrates the layout for both quilt backs. In each case, seams will run parallel to the top edge of the quilt.

Diagram 6

For the double-size quilt, cut the backing fabric into three equal lengths and trim the selvages. Cut a 30-inch-wide panel from the entire length of two segments, and sew a narrow panel to each side of

Double-Size Quilt Diagram

Queen-Size Quilt Diagram

the full-width piece. Press the seams open.

For the queen-size quilt, cut the backing fabric into three equal lengths and trim the selvages. Cut a 35-inch-wide panel from the entire length of two segments, and sew a narrow panel to each side of the full-width piece. Press the seams open.

Step 3. Layer the backing, batting, and quilt top. Baste the layers together. Quilt by hand or machine, adding any additional quilting designs of your choice as desired.

Step 4. Referring to the directions on page 121, make and attach double-fold binding to finish at a width of ¼ inch. To calculate the amount of binding you will need for the quilt size you are making, add the length of the four sides of the quilt plus 9 inches.

REFLECTIONS
Color Plan

Photocopy this page and use it to experiment with color schemes for your quilt.

BROKEN STAR

Skill Level: *Intermediate*

The Broken Star quilt pattern, a variation of the beloved Lone Star, was introduced by McCall's in 1920, and its dramatic beauty has stood the test of time. This particular version, pieced by Kathryn England, contains over 1,000 shimmering diamonds in cool blues, greens, and violets. But don't let the numbers fool you. The strip-piecing directions make cutting and assembly quicker than you'd think!

BEFORE YOU BEGIN

This quilt is assembled using quick-cutting and quick-piecing techniques. Six different strip sets are sewn, then angled segments are cut from each and sewn together to create the large diamonds that form the star points. Setting squares and triangles fill in the gaps around the star points, so if you are unfamiliar with sewing set-in seams, you may want to refer to "Setting In Pieces" on page 117 before beginning this project.

CHOOSING FABRICS

The quiltmaker used light, medium, and dark values of green, blue, and orchid in the quilt shown on the opposite page. The points on each end of the large diamonds are dark fabrics, and as they move inward to wider rows, patches shade from dark to light, and then back to dark again at the center of each of the diamonds.

This placement of color value links the diamonds and creates a radiating, circular-shaped star pattern from the center of the quilt outward. To develop a color scheme for the quilt that you are going to make, photocopy the **Color Plan** on page 41, and use colored pencils or crayons to experiment with different color arrangements.

Quilt Sizes

	Queen (shown)	King
Finished Quilt Size	95" × 95"	102" × 102"
Number of Large Diamonds	32	32
Finished Setting Square Size	12¾"	12¾"

Materials

Fabric	Queen	King
White-and-blue print	4¾ yards	5⅜ yards
Black-and-gray print	1¼ yards	1¼ yards
Medium blue print	1 yard	1 yard
Dark blue print	1 yard	1 yard
Light blue print	⅞ yard	⅞ yard
Light blue-and-gray print	⅞ yard	⅞ yard
Light green print	¾ yard	¾ yard
Light orchid print	¾ yard	¾ yard
Dark orchid print	¾ yard	¾ yard
Medium green print	½ yard	½ yard
Medium orchid print	½ yard	½ yard
Dark green print	¼ yard	¼ yard
Backing	8¾ yards	9¼ yards
Batting	102" × 102"	109" × 109"
Binding	⅝ yard	¾ yard

NOTE: Yardages are based on 44/45-inch-wide fabrics that are at least 42 inches wide after preshrinking.

Cutting Chart

Fabric	Used For	Strip Width	Strips Needed
White/blue print	Setting squares	13¼"	7
	Setting triangles	19¼"	1
	Outer border*	3¼"	9
■ Black/gray print	Strip sets	2"	18
■ Medium blue print	Strip sets	2"	15
■ Dark blue print	Strip sets	2"	15
■ Light blue print	Strip sets	2"	12
■ Light blue/gray print	Strip sets	2"	12
■ Light green print	Strip sets	2"	9
■ Light orchid print	Strip sets	2"	9
■ Dark orchid print	Strip sets	2"	3
	Inner border	1½"	9
■ Medium green print	Strip sets	2"	6
■ Medium orchid print	Strip sets	2"	6
■ Dark green print	Strip sets	2"	3

* The border strip widths are for the queen-size quilt. For the king-size quilt, cut ten 6¾-inch-wide strips from the white-and-blue print fabric for the outer border. Cut the same number and width strips for the inner border as for the queen-size quilt.

CUTTING

All measurements include ¼-inch seam allowances. Refer to the Cutting Chart for the number and dimensions of each piece or strip required for this quilt.

Note: We recommend that you piece one sample strip set and cut the star segments from it before cutting and stitching all strip sets.

• For the setting squares that surround the center star and fill in the corners of the quilt, cut the 13¼-inch white-and-blue print strips into twenty 13¼-inch squares.

• For the setting triangles that fill in the sides of the quilt, cut the 19¼-inch white-and-blue print strip into two 19¼-inch squares. Cut the squares in half diagonally in both directions. (This puts the more stable straight of grain at the edge of the quilt and helps eliminate stretching.)

MAKING THE STRIP SETS

To quick-piece the large diamonds that make up the center star and the broken star that surrounds it, you will make strip sets that will be cut into segments of joined small diamonds. These rows of small diamonds will be stitched together to form the large diamonds.

Step 1. To make Strip Set A, sew together strips in the order shown in **Diagram 1**. Stagger the strips by approximately 1½ inches, as shown. Press all the seams toward the dark green strip, as indicated by the arrow. Make three of Strip Set A.

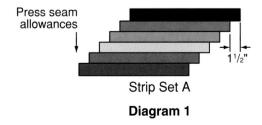

Press seam allowances

Strip Set A

Diagram 1

Step 2. Use a rotary cutter and a ruler with a 45 degree angle marking to cut 2-inch-wide segments from the strip set. First, position the ruler so that the 45 degree angle line is parallel to one of the seam lines in your strip set, then trim off the staggered edges of one end, as shown in **Diagram 2A**.

Then, slide the ruler over so that the 2-inch marking is aligned with the edge you just cut and the 45 degree line is still parallel to the seam line, as shown in **2B**. Cut a 2-inch segment from the strip set. Continue cutting 2-inch-wide segments from the three strip sets until you have 32 Strip Set A segments.

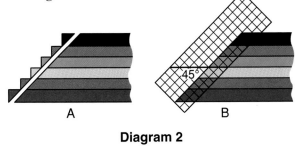

Diagram 2

each strip set in the direction of the arrow so assembling the large diamonds will be easier.

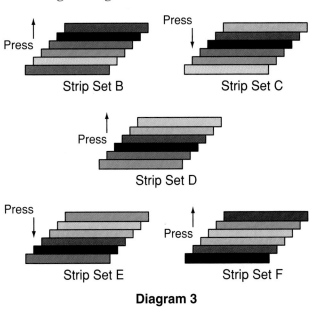

Diagram 3

Sew Easy

To make sure all of your diamonds are truly diamond-shaped, be sure to align the 45 degree line with the strip set seams. If you notice it's not quite lining up as you measure and cut your segments, realign it perfectly and trim off some of the diagonal edge of the strip set before measuring your next segment. Don't worry about wasting ¼ inch or so of fabric after every few cuts to straighten your strip sets. The little bit of waste you trim off will ensure that each strip segment is accurate.

ASSEMBLING THE DIAMONDS

Step 1. To make a large diamond, sew one segment from each type of strip set together, as shown in **Diagram 4**. Match the seams carefully by pinning through the seam allowances ¼ inch from the raw edges. Notice that because the seams are angled at 45 degrees, the seam allowances will not butt together. Pin each seam allowance in place before stitching. Wait to press seam allowances.

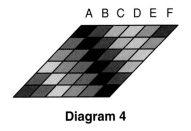

Diagram 4

Step 3. Make Strip Sets B, C, D, E, and F in the same manner, referring to **Diagram 3** for the color orders of those sets. Cut a total of 32 segments from each type of strip set, keeping like segments together. Be sure to press the seam allowances of

Step 2. Repeat, assembling a total of 32 identical large diamonds. Press the seams on half of the large diamonds toward the green small diamonds and press the seams on the other half of the large diamonds toward the orchid diamonds. This allows the diamonds to fit together more easily as you assemble the quilt top.

ASSEMBLING THE QUILT TOP

As you sew the components of this quilt together, do not sew into the seam allowances at the beginnings and ends of seams. These free seam allowances let you set in diamonds, squares, and triangles at angled intersections. For more information about set-in piecing, see page 117.

Sew Easy

To make sure you leave exactly ¼ inch open at each end of a diamond seam, mark the ¼ inch on your sewing machine throat plate with masking tape. Or, measure the seam allowances on each diamond end and mark them with a pencil dot. These guides tell you exactly where to start and stop sewing.

The Center Star

Step 1. Matching seams carefully, sew two large diamonds together, as shown in **Diagram 5A,** with the dark green patches aligned along the lower edge. Be sure to start sewing ¼ inch from the raw edges and backstitch. Likewise, stop sewing ¼ inch from the end of the seam and backstitch. Sew together another pair of large diamonds in the same manner, then join the pairs to create a half star, as shown in **5B.**

A

B

Diagram 5

Step 2. Repeat Step 1 to make another half star. Sew the two halves together, as shown in **Diagram 6.** Press all seams to one side so they fan out around the star.

Diagram 6

Step 3. Set a white-and-blue 13¼-inch square into each opening around the star, as shown.

Sew Easy

When setting in squares around the center star, align the edges of the star points precisely with the side of each square. Avoid problems with stretchy bias by matching and pinning the ends first, then pinning at each seam to ease in any fullness. To match the ends, poke a pin through the ¼-inch seam allowance of both the square and the diamond. The tip of the end diamond will extend beyond the edge of the square, as shown.

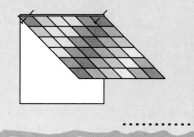

The Broken Star

Step 1. Sew together three large diamonds, matching seams carefully and aligning the dark orchid small diamonds to meet at the unit's center, as shown in **Diagram 7.** Leave the seam allowance open ¼ inch at the outer edges (the black diamonds) to accommodate the final setting squares. Repeat, making a total of eight sets of three diamonds.

Diagram 7

Step 2. Set a group of three diamonds into each opening between setting squares on the center star, as shown in the **Assembly Diagram** on page 40.

Step 3. To complete a quilt corner, sew a setting square to the outer diamond edges, as shown in the upper right corner of the **Assembly Diagram.** Sew two more setting squares together, and set them in next to the previous setting square, again referring to the upper right corner of the diagram. Press seam allowances toward the squares. Repeat for the remaining three corners.

Step 4. Sew setting triangles into the remaining openings, aligning raw edges and stitching from the outer edges toward the quilt center. Stop ¼ inch from the end of the seam and backstitch. Repeat for the other seam of each triangle. Press the seam allowances toward the triangles.

ADDING THE BORDERS

This quilt has a narrow, dark orchid inner border and a wider, white-and-blue print outer border.

Step 1. Measure the width of the quilt through the horizontal center, rather than along an edge. Sew the 1½-inch dark orchid border strips together end to end to achieve two borders this exact length to make top and bottom borders.

If you love the Lone Star at the heart of this quilt design and don't have time to piece a bed-size quilt, make just the center! Replace the top, bottom, and side setting squares with setting triangles for a square wallhanging, as shown below. Cut the setting triangles as described in the Cutting Chart for the outer section of the Broken Star. You'll need four setting triangles and four setting squares for this size quilt. Add borders to your liking or take a shortcut and just quilt and bind.

Substitute setting triangles

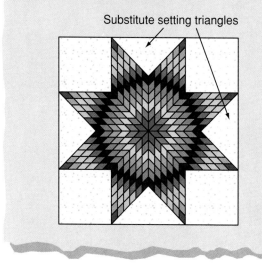

Step 2. Fold one border strip in half crosswise and crease. Unfold it and position it right side down along the top of the quilt, with the crease at the vertical midpoint. Pin at the midpoint and ends first, then across the width of the entire quilt, easing in fullness if necessary. Sew the border to the quilt. Repeat on the bottom of the quilt. Press seam allowances toward the borders.

Step 3. Measure the length of the quilt through the vertical center, including the top and bottom borders. Sew the remaining 1½-inch dark orchid border strips together end to end to make two side borders this exact length. Attach the side borders in the same manner as you did for the top and bottom borders.

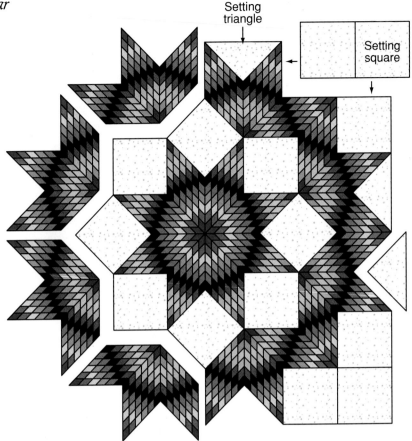

Setting triangle

Setting square

Assembly Diagram

Step 4. Following the directions in Steps 1 through 3, calculate lengths for the outer border strips. Piece together the white-and-blue strips as necessary, and sew them to the quilt as directed above. Press the seams toward the dark orchid border to prevent show-through.

QUILTING AND FINISHING

Step 1. Mark the top for quilting. In the quilt shown, the large diamonds are outline quilted. The background areas are quilted with a variety of feather and heart motifs.

Step 2. To make the quilt backing for either size quilt, cut the backing fabric into three equal segments and trim the selvages. For the queen-size quilt, cut a 31-inch-wide panel from the entire length of two of the pieces, then sew them to either side of the full-width piece, as shown in **Diagram 8.** For the king-size quilt, cut a 35-inch-

wide panel from the entire length of two of the pieces, then sew them to the full-width piece. Press the seams open.

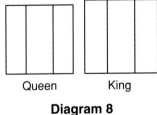

Queen   King

Diagram 8

Step 3. Layer the backing, batting, and quilt top. Baste the layers together. Quilt by hand or machine, adding additional quilting as desired.

Step 4. Referring to the directions on page 121, make and attach double-fold binding. To make the ½-inch binding shown in the photo, cut your binding strips 2½ inches wide. To calculate the amount of binding you will need, add up the length of the four sides of the quilt plus 9 inches.

BROKEN STAR
Color Plan

Photocopy this page and use it to experiment with color schemes for your quilt.

FEATHERED WORLD WITHOUT END

Skill Level: *Challenging*

◆

ere's a quilt that positively glows! Valerie Schadt of Fayetteville, New York, teams the traditional World without End and the classic Feathered Star and gives new life to both with a selection of carefully placed and decidedly nontraditional fabrics. Our easy-to-follow foundation method allows you to piece this stunner with minimal fuss and maximum accuracy.

BEFORE YOU BEGIN

Although this quilt *is* challenging, with its many small pieces and set-in seams, foundation piecing makes it easy to achieve accurate results. The block is assembled as a series of three different units, which are pieced over paper foundations. These foundations are then sewn together to construct the blocks. To complete the quilt, large diamonds are set into the angles between the blocks.

Preparing foundations does take time, but there are benefits to offset the extra preparation. Since there is no need to cut pieces to exact sizes, cutting time is greatly decreased. If you position pieces correctly and sew carefully on the marked lines, you'll find that the finished units fit together perfectly.

To make the task even easier, we've included lots of tips and illustrations along with our usual step-by-step instructions. If you haven't tried foundation piecing, be sure to read through the instructions carefully before beginning this project.

If you are new to the process and would like to try foundation

piecing on a small scale, we've given directions to make a wall-hanging version of this design. Try the larger quilt if you are an experienced foundation piecer or if you're feeling up to the challenge of a more ambitious project.

Although not quite large enough to qualify as a true bedspread, it is the perfect decorative cover for a double or queen bed when paired with a dust ruffle and pillow shams—hence our designation as bed topper.

Quilt Sizes		
	Wallhanging	Bed Topper (shown)
Finished Quilt Size	40" × 40"	72" × 72"
Finished Block Size	16"	16"
Number of Blocks	4	16

Materials		
Fabric	Wallhanging	Bed Topper
Assorted dark, light, and medium prints and solids	1¾ yards	5 yards
Medium yellow solid	1⅛ yards	1⅞ yards
Very light yellow solid	⅝ yard	⅝ yard
Deep gold mottled print or solid	⅜ yard	⅝ yard
Dark yellow solid	*	2½ yards
Light yellow solid	*	1¼ yards
Backing	2¾ yards	4½ yards
Batting	47" × 47"	79" × 79"
Binding	⅜ yard	⅝ yard

NOTE: *Yardages are based on 44/45-inch-wide fabrics that are at least 42 inches wide after preshrinking.*

* *Light yellow and dark yellow solid fabrics are not required for the wallhanging.*

Cutting Chart

Fabric	Used For	Strip Width or Pieces	Number to Cut Wallhanging	Bed Topper
Assorted lights, mediums, and darks	F	3½" squares	4	16
	G	3⅛" squares	8	32
	H	4" squares	8	32
	Feathers for Foundations B, C	2"	*	*
Assorted lights and mediums	Large triangle for Foundation C	3¾"	*	*
Medium yellow	D	Template D	8	12
Very light yellow	D	Template D	4	4
Gold	E	Template E	4	12
Dark yellow	D	Template D	—	16
Light yellow	D	Template D	—	8

* You may wish to wait to cut these strips until you begin piecing the Foundation B and C units. This will allow you to determine how many strips you wish to cut from each fabric. As a rule of thumb, the Foundation B and C units for each block will require approximately two 2-inch-wide light and two 2-inch-wide dark strips for the feathers, and one 3¾-inch-wide strip for the large triangle pieces. These strips can be uniform within the block, or completely scrappy.

Refer to "Quiltmaking Basics," beginning on page 112, for techniques to assist you with this project.

CHOOSING FABRICS

The blocks in this quilt are pieced in warm and scrappy combinations of red, orange, and yellow. Blue—whether pale or deep—provides the cool contrast. The placement of lights and darks varies from block to block, with one notable exception. All of the diamond star tips are very dark prints, which creates a secondary star motif and enhances the illusion of curves in the design.

While the tiny triangles or "feathers" do not need to be so consistently dark, it is important for them to stand out from the block backgrounds. To achieve this contrast, keep the background fabrics fairly light in value and relatively subtle in terms of print.

You can make the blocks in this quilt as uniform or as scrappy as you please. This quiltmaker has pieced all of the Foundation B and C units in a single block from the same group of fabrics, but each block is different from its neighbor. She's included lots of "surprise" fabrics to give the traditional pattern up-to-the-minute appeal.

In the quilt shown, the large diamonds separating the blocks progress from the lightest yellow in the center to dark yellow as you move toward the quilt's perimeter. Deep gold half-diamonds finish the outer edges of the quilt. Whether you choose yellow or another color for the diamonds, it is important that you maintain this light-to-dark progression in order to give the quilt its "lit from within" appearance.

To develop your own color scheme, photocopy the **Color Plan** on page 55, and use crayons or colored pencils to experiment with different color arrangements.

CUTTING

All measurements include ¼-inch seam allowances. For easy reference, the **Block Diagram**, the **Foundations Diagram**, and the **Assembly Diagrams** on pages 50 and 51 are all keyed to identify the various pieces and units by letter or name. Refer to the Cutting Chart and cut the required number of strips and pieces in the sizes needed. Cut all strips across the width of the fabric (crosswise grain).

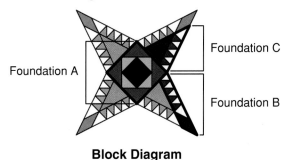

Block Diagram

Make templates for pieces D and E from the patterns and instructions on page 52. For more information about making templates, see page 116.

You will need to cut some of the squares into triangles for the Foundation A units, as follows:

• For the G triangles, cut each print and solid 3⅛-inch square in half once diagonally.

• For the H triangles, cut each of the assorted print and solid 4-inch squares in half once diagonally.

Note: We recommend that you cut and piece a sample block before cutting all of the fabric for the quilt.

Block Component Chart

	Wallhanging	Bed Topper
Number of Foundation A Units	4	16
Number of Foundation B Units	16	64
Number of Foundation C Units	16	64

When a pattern requires larger-than-usual templates, such as the D and E setting diamonds in this design, freezer paper makes a good, inexpensive choice for template material. The freezer paper template can be pressed directly onto the fabric, then removed and reused a number of times before it requires replacement. Fabric can be stacked to cut more than one layer at a time, saving additional time and money. Cut carefully so that you do not slice away slivers of the paper pattern.

PIECING THE FEATHERED STARS

Each block in this quilt requires one Foundation A unit, four Foundation B units, and four Foundation C units. The **Foundations Diagram** is labeled to identify the three different foundation units and their various component parts.

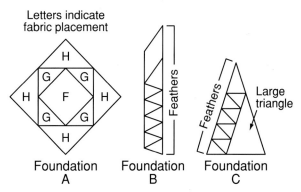

Foundations Diagram

Preparing the Foundations

Before you begin piecing, you need to prepare all of the base foundations required for the quilt. Refer to the Block Component Chart and trace the required number of Foundation A, B, and C units from the pattern on page 52.

Although foundations can be made from either fabric or paper, we recommend that you use paper foundations for this quilt. The weight and stability of the paper helps to prevent the stretching and distortion that sometimes occurs with fabric foundations. In addition, paper is comparatively inexpensive and readily available.

Many types of paper are suitable for foundations. Newsprint is an excellent choice because it is sturdy enough to hold up to handling and stitching, but it tears away easily after the quilt is finished. Blank newsprint is available from office supply stores in pads of many sizes, so it is easy to draft large patterns (larger than a copier can reproduce). Other possible choices include onion skin paper, tracing paper, and copier paper.

One method to avoid tracing each pattern individually is to use a hot iron transfer pen. Draw the full-size image onto tracing paper, then iron it onto the foundation paper. The image can usually be ironed onto a foundation material five or six times. Retrace the original transfer for additional ironings, taking care to mark over the existing lines exactly. It's a good idea to piece one block before making all your copies.

A photocopier can also be used to duplicate your foundations, but you need to take the following precautions to be sure that you don't distort your patterns:

• Make sure the copier is set to reproduce the image at exactly 100 percent.

• Use only the original drawing from the book to make photocopies. Copies of copies are more likely to become distorted.

• Compare each copy with the original pattern. If you find you are having problems with distortion, position the original pattern as close to the center of the copied page as possible. This will often eliminate the distortion.

Piecing on a Foundation

If you look at Foundations A through C on pages 53–54, you'll see that the only seam allowance included is the one around the outer perimeter of the pattern. The outer line will eventually be the cutting line and will allow you to ac-

curately trim away excess fabric once the unit is pieced. All other lines on the foundation are sewing lines. Seam allowances are created when you overlap pieces for sewing. The foundations are not removed until the entire quilt is assembled.

Try to follow the same guidelines for grain placement that you would normally use when piecing. When possible, the fabric straight of grain should be parallel with the outer edge of the block.

Cut out each paper foundation prior to piecing, adding at least ¼ inch of additional paper around all the sides.

Although it's not a critical point for symmetrical patterns like Foundation A, keep in mind that the printed sides of the asymmetrical B and C foundations are a mirror image of how the finished unit will look.

Piecing the Foundation A Units

Step 1. The Foundation A unit forms the square-within-a-square at the center of each block. Position a 3½-inch F square right side up on the reverse (unprinted) side of the foundation, centering it over the lines for piece 1, as shown in **Diagram 1**. To check placement, hold the foundation up to the light, with the printed side away from you. The edges of the fabric should overlap the seam lines for the center patch. Hold the square in place with a pin or a dab of glue stick.

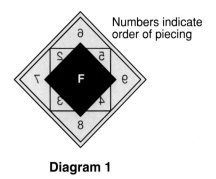

Diagram 1

Step 2. Select four G triangles to surround the center square. These triangles can be cut from the same fabric, or they can be totally scrappy. To sew piece 2, place a G triangle right side down on the

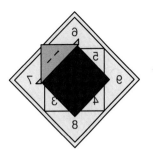

Diagram 3

reverse side of the foundation, aligning its longest edge with one side of the center F square, as shown in **Diagram 2A**. Secure the triangle in place, and turn to the printed side of the foundation. Using a stitch length of 14 to 18 stitches per inch, sew directly on the line that separates piece 1 from piece 2, beginning and ending the seam approximately ⅛ inch on either side of the line, as shown in **2B**.

Step 4. To add piece 3, place another G triangle right side down, aligning its longest edge with the center square, as shown in **Diagram 4A**. Turn to the printed side of the foundation, and sew directly on the line that separates piece 1 from piece 3, beginning and ending the seam approximately ⅛ inch on either side of the line, as shown in **4B**. Turn the foundation over and trim, flip, finger press, and pin as you did previously.

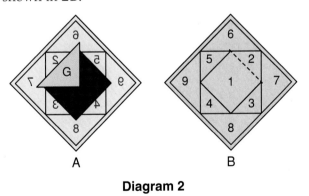

Diagram 2

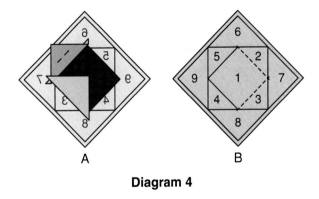

Diagram 4

Step 3. Turn to the reverse side of the foundation. Trim the excess seam allowance between the newly sewn patches if necessary, then flip the triangle into a right side up position. Finger press and pin in place. The reverse side of the foundation should resemble **Diagram 3**. Make sure the short sides of the triangle overlap the seam lines around its outer edges by enough to create a stable seam allowance when those seams are sewn.

Step 5. Add pieces 4 and 5 in the same manner, trimming seam allowances and finger pressing each in place. The unprinted side of the foundation should now resemble **Diagram 5**.

Diagram 5

Step 6. Select four H triangles to complete the outer ring of the Foundation A unit. These triangles may all be cut from the same fabric, or may be totally scrappy. Place a triangle right side down on the pieced unit, aligning its longest edge as shown in **Diagram 6A.** Use the intersection of pieces 2 and 5 as a guide to placement. Make sure the long edge of the new piece (piece 6) overlaps the seam by approximately ¼ inch. Turn to the printed side of the foundation, and sew on the line separating pieces 2 and 5 from piece 6. Flip piece 6 right side up, finger pressing it in place. The reverse side of the foundation should resemble **6B.**

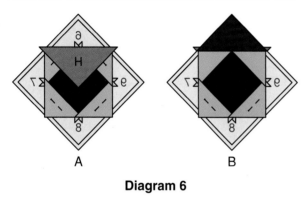

Diagram 6

Step 7. Add the remaining H triangles as described in Step 6, working around all sides of the pieced unit. When all four are sewn to the foundation, press it lightly on the pieced side. Turn it over and use scissors or a rotary cutter to cut on the outermost lines, trimming away excess fabric. The unit is a perfect square-in-a-square with a ¼-inch seam allowance surrounding it.

Step 8. Repeat to assemble one Foundation A unit for each block in your quilt.

Piecing the Foundation B Units

Step 1. To piece a Foundation B unit, select dark and light 2½-inch-wide strips from the fabrics cut for feathers. Place a dark strip right side up on the reverse side of the foundation, covering all of piece 1, as shown in **Diagram 7A.** Be sure all edges of the strip extend past the seam lines. Place a light strip right side down on top of it and pin it in place, as shown in **7B.**

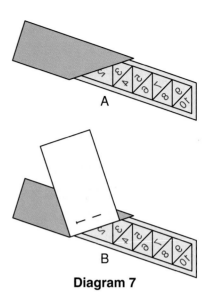

Diagram 7

Step 2. Turn to the printed side of the foundation and sew on the line separating piece 1 from piece 2, stopping and starting approximately ⅛ inch on either side of the line, as shown in **Diagram 8A.** Turn to the reverse side and trim away the excess seam allowance and any extra tails of fabric. Finger press piece 2 into a right side up position and pin. The pieced side of the foundation should resemble **8B.**

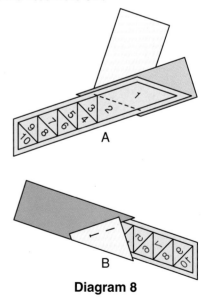

Diagram 8

Step 3. To add piece 3, position a dark strip face down on top of piece 2 as shown in **Diagram 9A.** Secure the fabric and turn to the printed side

of the foundation. Sew on the line separating piece 2 from piece 3. Flip, trim, finger press, and pin, as shown in **9B**. Add all remaining pieces in the same manner. When you reach the end of the strip, press the pieced side of the foundation lightly, then use scissors or a rotary cutter to trim on the outermost line of the foundation.

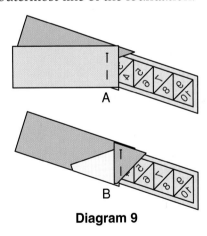

Diagram 9

Step 4. Repeat Steps 1 through 3 to assemble four Foundation B units for each block.

Piecing the Foundation C Units

Step 1. Foundation C is assembled in basically the same manner as Foundation B. Begin at piece 1 with a light strip, then alternate darks and lights until you reach piece 9. The triangles are sewn in the opposite direction as those in Foundation B, so that seams will be pressed in opposite directions when the pieces are joined.

Step 2. To add piece 10, position a 3¾-inch-wide strip of medium value fabric right side down on the reverse side of the foundation, as shown in **Diagram 10**. Flip the foundation over to the printed side, and sew on the line separating piece 10 from the light and dark triangles. Trim the excess fabric and seam allowances, and flip and finger press piece 10 in place. Press the unit on the pieced side, and trim on the outermost line of the foundation.

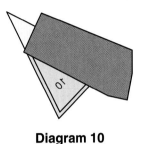

Diagram 10

Step 3. Repeat Steps 1 and 2 to assemble four Foundation C units for each block in your quilt.

ASSEMBLING THE BLOCK

Step 1. Set your sewing machine to its normal stitch length. Matching seams carefully, sew a Foundation B unit to a Foundation C unit, as shown in **Diagram 11** on page 50. The foundation papers provide a good guide when matching pieces, but be sure to check individual seam placement. Repeat, connecting all B and C foundations in the same manner.

Diagram 11

Step 2. Sew a Foundation B/C unit to one side of a Foundation A unit, as shown in **Diagram 12A.** Begin ¼ inch from the raw edge at the foundation's marked seam, take three stitches, and backstitch, taking care not to stitch back into the seam allowance. Complete the seam, ending with a backstitch ¼ inch from the raw edge, at the end of the marked seam line. Sew the remaining three Foundation B/C units to the other three sides of Foundation A in the same manner to complete the block, as shown in **12B.**

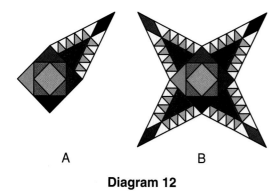

A   B

Diagram 12

Step 3. Repeat Steps 1 and 2 to assemble the required number of blocks for your quilt.

ASSEMBLING THE QUILT

Step 1. Use a design wall or other flat surface to arrange the blocks, as shown in the **Wallhanging** and **Bed Topper Assembly Diagrams.** Place the large yellow D diamonds between the blocks, as shown. The lightest yellow diamonds will be at the center of the quilt, with the diamonds be-

coming progressively darker as you move toward the outer edges. Place the gold E half-diamonds around the outer edges of the quilt. Refer to the photograph on page 42 as needed.

Step 2. Sew the vertical D diamonds to the sides of the blocks, as indicated in the **Wallhanging** and **Bed Topper Assembly Diagrams,** pivoting to set in the pieces. For additional instructions on set-in seams, see page 117 in "Quiltmaking Basics."

Step 3. Set in the horizontal diamonds in the same manner. You will be connecting the rows as you work.

Step 4. Use the same method to set in the E half-diamonds to finish the edges of the quilt.

Step 5. Remove all foundation papers and press the quilt.

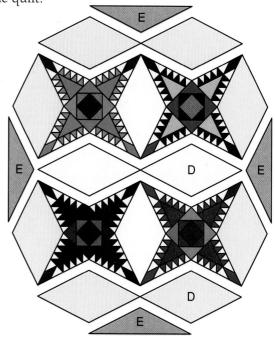

Wallhanging Assembly Diagram

QUILTING AND FINISHING

Step 1. Mark the top for quilting. The quilt shown was quilted with a stylized pineapple motif surrounded by leaves in the center of each block. The rest of the quilt is channel quilted.

Bed Topper Assembly Diagram

Step 2. Regardless of which quilt you are making, you will need to piece the backing. **Diagram 13** illustrates the layout for both size quilt backs.

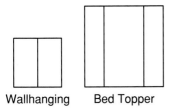

| Wallhanging | Bed Topper |

Diagram 13

For the wallhanging, cut the backing fabric in half crosswise and trim the selvages. Cut a 25-inch-wide panel from the entire length of each piece. Sew the two panels together lengthwise, as shown. Press the seam open.

For the topper, cut the backing fabric in half crosswise and trim the selvages. Cut two 20-inch-wide pieces from the entire length of one piece of backing fabric, and sew a narrow panel to each side of the full-width piece, as shown. Press the seams open.

Step 3. Layer the backing, batting, and quilt top, and baste the layers together. Quilt by hand or machine, adding additional quilting as desired.

Step 4. Referring to the directions on page 121 in "Quiltmaking Basics," make and attach double-fold binding to finish at a width of ¼ inch. To calculate the amount of binding you will need for the quilt size you are making, add the length of the four sides of the quilt plus 9 inches.

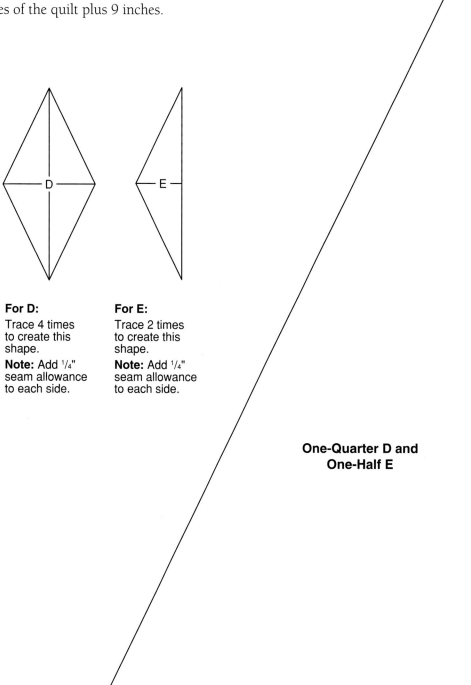

For D:
Trace 4 times to create this shape.

Note: Add ¼" seam allowance to each side.

For E:
Trace 2 times to create this shape.

Note: Add ¼" seam allowance to each side.

One-Quarter D and One-Half E

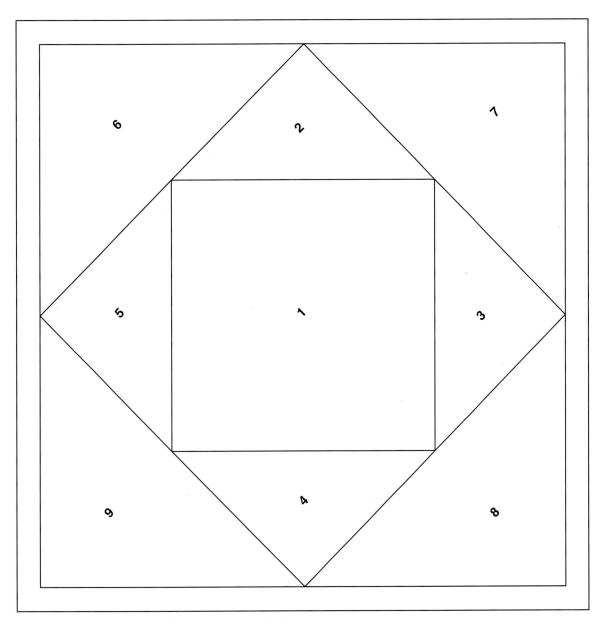

Foundation A

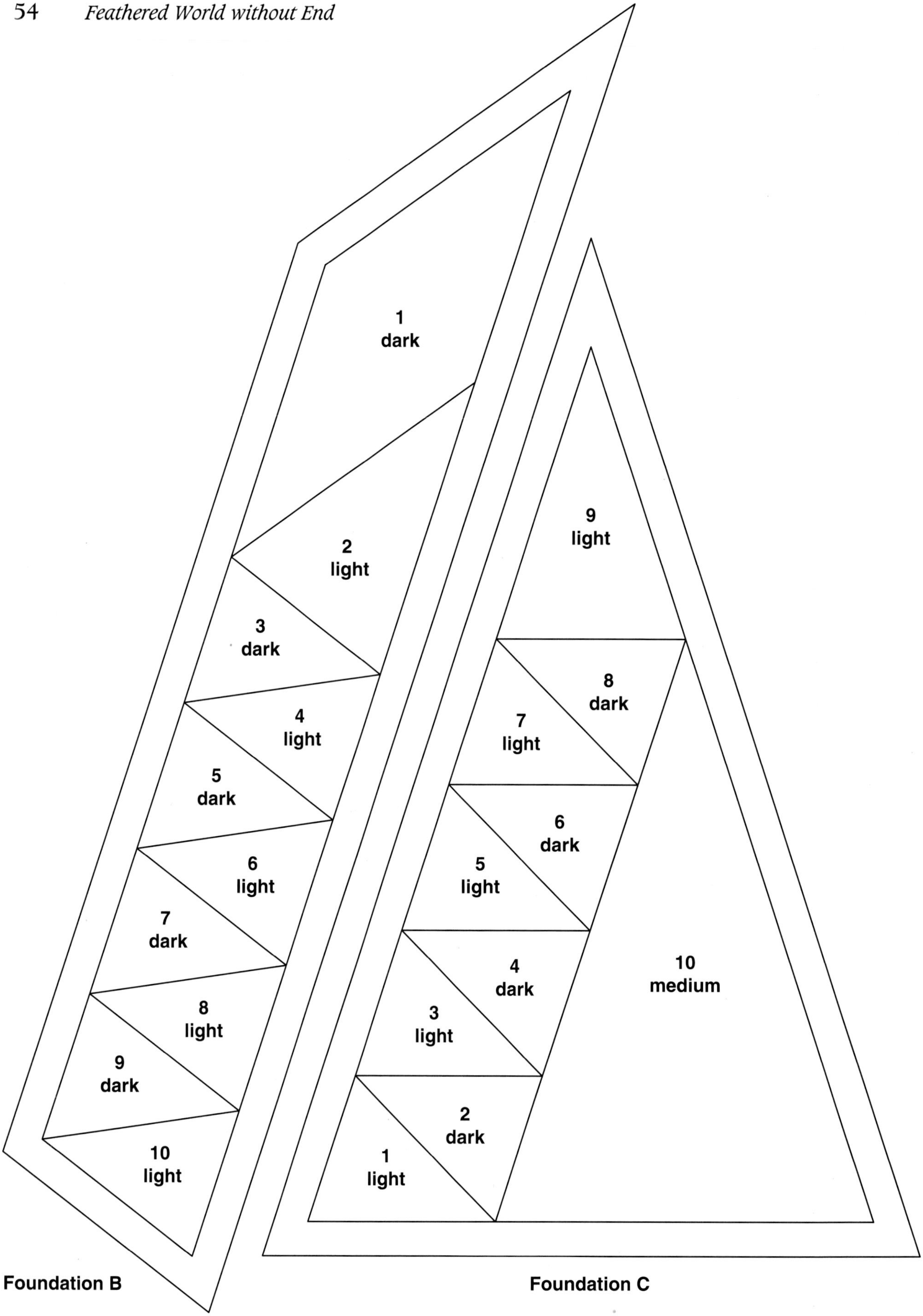

1
dark

2
light

3
dark

4
light

5
dark

6
light

7
dark

8
light

9
dark

10
light

9
light

8
dark

7
light

6
dark

5
light

4
dark

3
light

2
dark

1
light

10
medium

Foundation B

Foundation C

FEATHERED WORLD WITHOUT END

Color Plan

Photocopy this page and use it to experiment with color schemes for your quilt.

Trailing Starflower

Skill Level: *Easy*

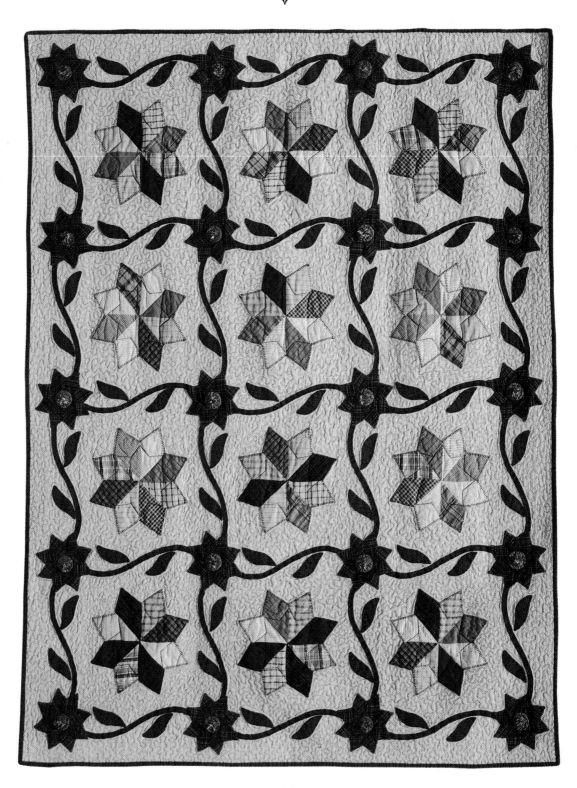

A cheerful mix of stars, flowers, and heartwarming plaids lends this small quilt a charming folk art feel. Quiltmaker Bethany S. Reynolds of Ellsworth, Maine, works visual magic using simple appliqué, colorful embroidery floss, and the nostalgic touch of yo-yos to enhance her homespun garden.

BEFORE YOU BEGIN

This project allows you to try a wide variety of quiltmaking techniques. You'll use both templates and your rotary cutter to cut the pieces. Construction methods include piecing, appliqué, making yo-yos, quilting, and tying. You can even try decorative hand or machine stitching for additional embellishment.

You might think such a variety of techniques would earn this quilt an intermediate or challenging rating. Not so! In fact, it offers the perfect opportunity for a confident beginner to sharpen skills in many areas. The piecing is easy, with stars and starflowers appliquéd to the background blocks, eliminating set-in seams. The appliqué pieces are few, and the shapes are simple. And the yo-yos and other embellishing techniques are just plain fun!

You may wish to read "Stars Basics," beginning on page 104, and "Quiltmaking Basics," beginning on page 112, before you begin this quilt. In addition to specific instructions about making and using templates, and using rotary cutters, you'll find lots of hints and tips to help with your appliqué technique.

Quilt Sizes

	Wallhanging	Lap (shown)
Finished Quilt Size	40½" × 40½"	56½" × 72½"
Finished Star Block Size	12"	12"
Number of Large Star Blocks	4	12
Number of Small Starflowers	9	20

Materials

Fabric	Wallhanging	Lap
Light solid or subtle print	1⅝ yards	3¾ yards
Dark green plaid	¾ yard	1 yard
Dark red plaid	⅝ yard	1⅜ yards
Assorted light plaids *(total)*	⅓ yard	⅝ yard
Assorted dark plaids *(total)*	⅓ yard	⅝ yard
Medium blue plaid	⅛ yard	¼ yard
Embroidery floss *(six-strand)*	2 skeins	2 skeins
Backing	2¾ yards	3¾ yards
Batting	48" × 48"	64" × 80"
Binding	⅓ yard	½ yard

NOTE: Yardages are based on 44/45-inch-wide fabrics that are at least 42 inches wide after preshrinking.

CHOOSING FABRICS

This quiltmaker has chosen to work almost exclusively in homespun and madras plaids. For the background, sashing, and borders, she has selected a gray, linen-weave cotton to enhance the folk art appearance of the quilt. As a substitute, you might select any light solid or subtle "reads-as-solid" cotton print in a neutral shade.

Light and dark value plaids alternate in the points of the large

Cutting Chart

Fabric	Used For	Strip Width or Pieces	Number to Cut Wallhanging	Lap	Second Cut Dimensions	Number to Cut Wallhanging	Lap
Light solid or subtle print	Borders	2½"	4	7			
	Block backgrounds	12½"	2	4	12½" squares	4	12
	Sashing strips	4½"	4	11	4½" × 12½"	12	31
	Corner squares	4½"	1	3	4½" squares	9	20
Dark green plaid	Vine	24" square	1	—			
		36" square	—	1			
	D*	Template D	24	62			
Dark red plaid	B	Template B	72	160			
Assorted light plaids	A	Template A	16	48			
Assorted dark plaids	A	Template A	16	48			
Medium blue plaid	C	Template C	9	20			

* After cutting vines from squares, cut leaves from leftovers before cutting additional fabric.

stars. For a scrappy look, select as many different plaids as possible. Neither lights nor darks need to be identical in value. Since the perceived value of a fabric is dependent on the value of its neighboring fabrics, some of your plaids may do "double duty" as both lights and darks. For more information about fabric value, see page 106 in "Stars Basics."

In the quilt shown, the vines and leaves are all sewn from the same dark green plaid. The small starflowers are a deep red-and-black plaid, with medium blue plaid yo-yo centers.

While the concentration of homespuns and plaids creates a cozy, country look, the design would be equally attractive in a colorful mix of plaids, stripes, and prints. Or you might prefer to focus solely on the wonderful reproduction prints currently available, including the soft pastels of the 1920s and 30s.

To develop your own color scheme for this quilt, photocopy the **Color Plan** on page 65, and use crayons or colored pencils to experiment with different color arrangements.

CUTTING

The pieces for this quilt are cut using a combination of templates and rotary-cutting techniques. Make templates for pieces A, B, C, and D from the full-size patterns on page 64. Refer to page 116 of "Quiltmaking Basics" for complete details on making and using templates.

With the exception of pattern pieces C and D, all of the full-size pattern pieces and the rotary-cutting measurements given include ¼-inch seam allowances. Refer to the Cutting Chart for the number of pieces or strips to cut from each fabric. Cut all strips across the width of the fabric (crosswise grain).

Note: We recommend that you cut and piece a sample block before cutting all of the fabric for your quilt.

PIECING THE LARGE STARS

Before you begin piecing the large stars, you may wish to trim the inner point of the A pieces to reduce bulk and allow for easier piecing. See "Sew Easy" on page 6 for details on trimming.

Step 1. Select four light A star points and four dark A star points. Position them as shown in the **Block Diagram**, alternating light and dark points.

Block Diagram

Step 2. Pin a light A piece to a dark A piece with right sides together. Sew the pieces together, beginning and ending with a backstitch exactly ¼ inch from each end, as indicated by the dots in **Diagram 1A**. Be careful not to sew into the ¼-inch seam allowance. Finger press the seam allowance toward the dark point. Your unit should look like **1B**.

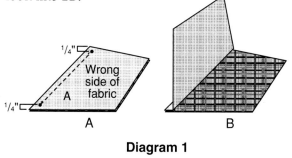

Diagram 1

Step 3. Repeat, sewing together the remaining three pairs of light and dark A star points.

Step 4. Sew two of the pairs together. Begin sewing ¼ inch from the edge, as shown by the dot in **Diagram 2A**, and backstitch. Continue sewing to the other dot (where the previously sewn seam ends). End with a backstitch. This unit should look like the one in **2B**. Finger press the seam allowance in the same direction as the others. Join the two remaining pairs to assemble the other half of the star.

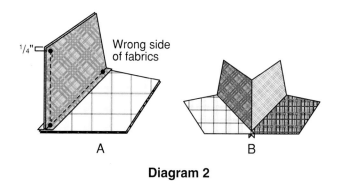

Diagram 2

Step 5. Pin the two star halves together with right sides facing. Rather than sewing completely across the star from one side to the other, begin stitching ¼ inch from one edge of the star and sew toward the center, stopping exactly at the point where all of the seams meet, as shown in **Diagram 3A**. Finger press the seam allowances out of the way. Sew the remaining seam, starting ¼ inch from the opposite side of the star, and sewing again only to the star center, as shown. Press the final seam in the same direction, fanning out the star center, as shown in **3B**.

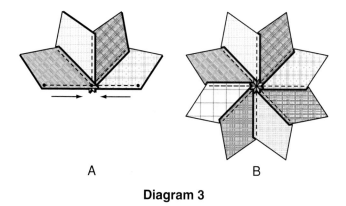

Diagram 3

Step 6. Repeat Steps 1 through 5 to assemble the number of large stars required for your quilt.

APPLIQUÉING THE LARGE STARS

In this quilt, the large stars are appliquéd onto, rather than pieced into, a background square. Refer to page 117 in "Quiltmaking Basics" for general information on appliqué.

Step 1. Use your preferred method to prepare all of the large stars for appliqué. If you use the needle-turn method, no additional preparation is necessary. If you prefer to turn the seam allowances in advance, turn under and baste the ¼-inch seam allowance you have left "free" around the outer edge of the star.

Step 2. Center a star on a 12½-inch background square. Appliqué the star to the square. Repeat to appliqué the required number of large Star blocks for your quilt.

── Sew Easy ──

Here's an easy way to position an appliqué motif in the center of a background square. Fold the square in half and carefully finger crease to mark the vertical center. Open the square, then refold in the opposite direction, finger creasing to mark the horizontal center. In the same manner, fold and crease both diagonal lines. The two creases will intersect at the exact center of the block, plus serve as guides for aligning appliqué pieces.

PIECING THE SMALL STARFLOWERS

Each corner square in this quilt is adorned with a smaller version of the large star that appears in the basic quilt block. The little stars are called starflowers, and each is finished with a decorative yo-yo center. Follow Steps 2 through 5 in the instructions for "Piecing the Large Stars" to complete the required number of starflowers for your quilt. Use the dark red plaid B star points you have cut to make the starflowers. The starflowers will be appliquéd to the corner squares after the quilt top has been assembled.

Note: Before you begin piecing the starflowers, trim the inner point of template B to reduce bulk and allow for easier piecing. See "Sew Easy" on page 6 for details on trimming templates.

·········Sew Quick·········

If you are lucky enough to have a sewing machine with fancy decorative stitches, you may prefer to machine appliqué the Star blocks, starflowers, vines, and leaves. Try a blanket stitch and contrasting thread for a warm, homespun look.

Making the Yo-Yo Centers

Step 1. Thread a hand sewing needle with a length of thread that matches the yo-yo fabric. Double the thread and tie a knot at the end. Working with the right side of a blue C circle away from you, use the drawn line as a guide to turn over a ¼-inch seam allowance. Take a backstitch to secure the thread. Stitch a running stitch approximately ⅛ inch from the outer edge of the circle, turning and basting the ¼-inch seam as you work, as shown in **Diagram 4**. Stitch around the entire perimeter of the circle.

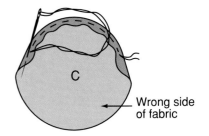

Wrong side of fabric

Diagram 4

Step 2. Draw up the thread to gather the edge tightly. Knot the thread and flatten the yo-yo at its center, as shown in **Diagram 5A**.

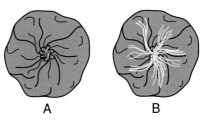

A   B

Diagram 5

Step 3. To make the stamens, thread a length of six-strand embroidery floss and take a stitch in the center hole of the yo-yo. Cut the floss, leaving approximately ¾ inch on both ends. Tie a double knot to secure. Repeat, making two more embroidery ties. Trim the threads so they are even, and untwist the strands, as shown in **5B**.

Step 4. Repeat Steps 1 through 3 to make the number of yo-yo centers required for the small starflowers in your quilt.

Step 5. Use a thread that matches the yo-yos to hand appliqué them to the centers of the starflowers, as shown in **Diagram 6.**

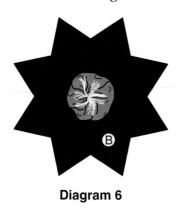

Diagram 6

Appliquéd Sashing

The sashing strips are appliquéd before they are sewn into the quilt top.

Making the Vines

We recommend that you use bias strips to make the gracefully curving vines for the sashing strips of your quilt. Refer to instructions on page 111 in "Stars Basics" for information on preparing bias strips. For the wallhanging, use the 24-inch square of dark green plaid to cut a total of twelve 24-inch-long bias strips. For the lap-size quilt, use the 36-inch square of dark green plaid to cut a total of 31 bias strips, each 24 inches long. Keep in mind that since the fabric is layered, each cut will yield two strips, and that some of these strips may be long enough to be divided into two 24-inch-long strips.

For either size quilt, cut the bias strips 1⅜ inches wide. Then fold, press, and sew the strips as instructed in "Appliquéing Leaves and Vines."

Preparing Leaves for Appliqué

Use your preferred method to prepare all leaves (D pieces) for appliqué. Refer to page 109 for information on freezer paper appliqué.

Appliquéing Leaves and Vines

Step 1. Gently shape a prepared vine to a 4½ × 12½-inch sashing strip, as shown in **Diagram 7.** Pin or baste in place.

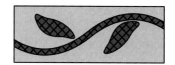

Diagram 7

Step 2. Pin or baste a leaf on each side of the vine, as shown in the diagram.

Step 3. Use your preferred method to appliqué the vine and leaves to the sashing strip. Trim away any excess vine that extends beyond the ends of the sashing strip.

Step 4. Repeat to appliqué the required number of sashing strips for your quilt.

Assembling the Quilt

Step 1. Use a design wall or other flat surface to arrange the Star blocks, sashing strips, and corner squares, as shown in the **Assembly Diagram** on page 62. Take care to position the appliqué sashing as shown. The wallhanging has two horizontal rows of two Star blocks each. The lap-size quilt has four horizontal rows of three Star blocks each.

Step 2. Sew the blocks, sashing strips, and corner squares into horizontal rows, as shown. Press seam allowances toward the sashing strips.

Step 3. Sew the rows together, matching seams carefully. Press the quilt.

Assembly Diagram

ADDING THE BORDERS

Step 1. Although the pre-cut, 2½ × 42-inch border strips are sufficient in length for the wall-hanging, you will need to piece strips to achieve the required lengths for the side and the top and bottom borders of the lap-size quilt. Cut one of the strips in half. Sew one full-length strip and one half strip together for the top and the bottom borders. Piece two of the 2½-inch-wide border strips end to end for each of the side borders.

Step 2. To determine the exact length for the side borders, measure the length of the quilt top, taking the measurement through its vertical center rather than along its sides. Trim the side border strips to this measurement.

Step 3. Fold a side border strip in half crosswise and crease. Unfold it and position it right side down along the side of the quilt, with its crease at the quilt's horizontal midpoint. Pin at the midpoint and ends first, then along the entire length of the quilt, easing in fullness if necessary. Sew the border to the quilt, and press the seam toward the border. Repeat on the opposite side of the quilt.

Step 4. Measure the width of the quilt, taking the measurement through its horizontal center rather than along the top or bottom edge, and including the side borders. Trim the top and bottom border strips to this measurement.

Step 5. Repeat the process described in Step 3 to attach the top and bottom borders to the quilt top.

APPLIQUÉING THE STARFLOWERS

Step 1. Center, then pin or baste a starflower on each corner square, as shown in the **Quilt Diagram.** The starflowers will overlap the squares and cover the ends of the vines.

Step 2. Use your preferred method to appliqué the starflowers to the quilt.

QUILTING AND FINISHING

Step 1. Mark the top for quilting. The quilt shown has been machine quilted. The large Star blocks have an offset star motif, as shown in **Diagram 8.** All other shapes are outlined, and the background is stipple quilted.

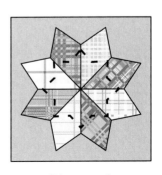

Diagram 8

Step 2. Regardless of which quilt size you've chosen to make, the backing will need to be pieced. **Diagram 9** illustrates the layout for both quilt backs.

Wallhanging Lap

Diagram 9

For the backing for the wallhanging, cut the backing fabric in half crosswise and trim the selvages. Cut a 24½-inch-wide panel from the entire length of each piece of backing fabric. Sew the two panels together lengthwise, and press the seam open. When you are layering the quilt top, batting, and backing for basting, turn the backing so that the seam is parallel to the top edge of the quilt, as shown in the diagram.

Wallhanging   Lap

Quilt Diagram

For the lap-size quilt, cut the backing fabric in half and trim the selvages. Trim each piece to 40 inches wide. Sew the two pieces together lengthwise, and press the seams open. When basting the quilt, the backing seam should be parallel to the top edge of the quilt, as shown in **Diagram 9** on page 63.

Step 3. Layer the backing, batting, and quilt top, and baste the layers together. Quilt by hand or machine, adding additional quilting designs of your choice as desired.

Step 4. Referring to the directions on page 121 in "Quiltmaking Basics," make and attach double-fold binding to finish at a width of $\frac{1}{4}$ inch. To calculate the amount of binding you will need for the quilt size you are making, add the length of the four sides of the quilt plus 9 inches.

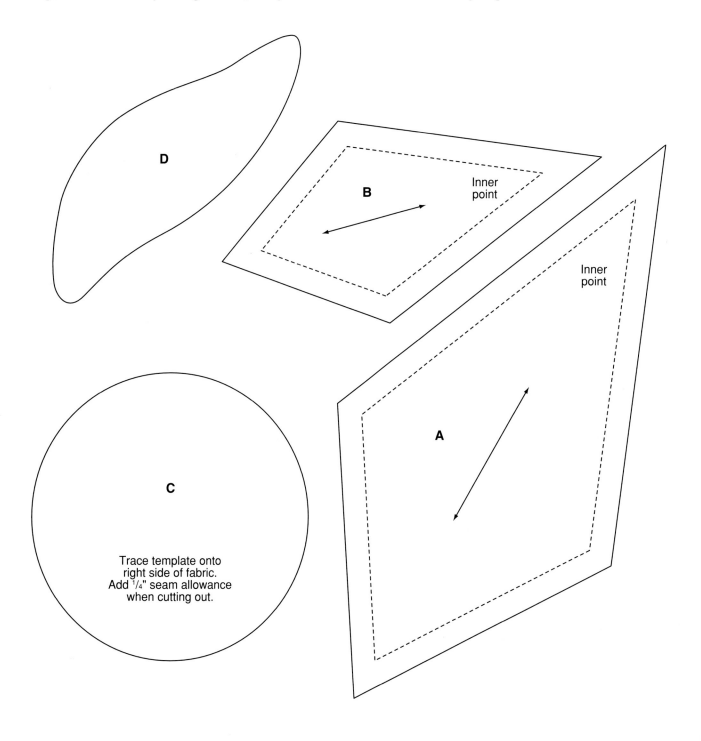

TRAILING STARFLOWER
Color Plan

Photocopy this page and use it to experiment with color schemes for your quilt.

SISTER'S CHOICE

Skill Level: *Intermediate*

The lovely Sister's Choice is a first cousin to the typical Star block, with its eight sparkling points and radiant image. This "garden-fresh" version is a true group effort, designed and assembled by Beverly Rogers. Members of the Kingwood (Texas) Area Quilt Guild stitched the jewel-tone blocks, and Dori Hawks added the crowning touch with her masterful machine quilting.

BEFORE YOU BEGIN

We've given this quilt an intermediate rating primarily because of the scope of the project and the appliqué border. Actually, the construction techniques are simple enough for a confident beginner to handle easily.

With the exception of a few appliqué pieces that require you to make and use templates, the entire quilt can be rotary cut. An efficient strip-piecing technique is included for you to use to construct the nine-patch centers for the Sister's Choice blocks, and the triangle squares are made using another quick-cutting, quick-piecing method that we describe for you.

Border vines are made from long bias strips, and you'll love the simple process and terrific results of freezer paper appliqué for preparing and stitching the flowers and leaves.

Refer to "Stars Basics" on page 104 and "Quiltmaking Basics" on page 112 for specific information and tips on rotary cutting, quick piecing, freezer paper appliqué, and a variety of other techniques that will help you as you work on this project.

Quilt Sizes

	Twin	Queen (shown)
Finished Quilt Size	65" × 89"	89" × 101"
Finished Block Size	10"	10"
Number of Blocks	24	42
Total Number of Nine Patches	24	42
Number of Triangle-Square Units*	192	336

You will need eight identical units for each block.

Materials

Fabric	Twin	Queen
White-on-white print	1⅔ yards	2⅛ yards
Assorted dark and bright jewel-tone prints (*total*)	1⅜ yards	2⅛ yards
Medium blue subtle print	1¼ yards	1⅞ yards
Light floral print	1⅛ yards	1⅞ yards
Assorted medium prints (*total*)	⅞ yard	1¼ yards
Royal blue solid or subtle print*	⅞ yard	1 yard
Dark green subtle print	¾ yard	⅞ yard
Dark green floral print	⅔ yard	1⅛ yards
Orchid batik print	⅓ yard	½ yard
Medium-dark green print	¼ yard	⅓ yard
Assorted green scraps (*total*)†	¼ yard	¼ yard
Backing	5½ yards	9 yards
Batting	72" × 96"	96" × 108"

NOTE: *Yardages are based on 44/45-inch-wide fabrics that are at least 42 inches wide after preshrinking.*

* *Includes binding.*

† *You may have enough leftovers from other greens to eliminate this yardage.*

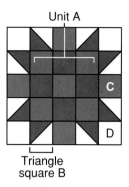

Block Diagram

Choosing Fabrics

The fabrics in this quilt suggest a garden in the riot of full bloom. While these quiltmakers have used just six different block colorations and arranged them in diagonal rows, the interesting mix of fabrics suggests a much scrappier quilt. In fact, to simplify construction, we are suggesting that you follow a similar color scheme, but take a somewhat more scrappy approach.

Refer to the quilt photo on page 66 and the **Block Diagram** at right. To achieve a look similar to the quilt shown, begin with a light background print. You'll want to choose an airy, open floral—not too busy—with lots of white space. This print will be used for the light triangle points (B) and the background squares (D) of each block, unifying all of the other prints.

Each block has a nine-patch center square (Unit A) composed of two fabrics. Choose a single dark green floral to appear in every block. Then select five or six medium-value floral fabrics in blue,

green, pink, purple, or other "garden" colors, so that you'll have a variety of different nine-patch units.

To complete each block, select a different jewel-tone color for the dark triangle points (B) and for the perimeter squares (C). Deep reds, teals, greens, purples, fuchsias, and electric blues all make wonderful choices. Focus on subtle, "reads-as-solid" or medium-scale floral prints for these shapes.

Carry the garden motif a step further by selecting a medium blue subtle print for the sashing

Fabric	Used For	Strip Width	Number to Cut Twin	Number to Cut Queen	Second Cut Dimensions	Number to Cut Twin	Number to Cut Queen
White-on-white print	Outer border	7"	8	10			
Batik	Inner border	1¼"	8	10			
Medium blue print	Sashing	2½"	15	25	2½" × 10½"	58	97
Medium dark green print	Corner squares	2½"	3	4	2½" squares	35	56
Light floral print	Triangle squares (B)	2⅞"	7	12	2⅞" squares	96	168
	D	2½"	6	11	2½" squares	96	168
Assorted medium prints	Nine patches	2½"	7	12			
Dark green floral print	Nine patches	2½"	8	15			
Assorted dark jewel-tone prints	Triangle squares (B)	2⅞"	7	12	2⅞" squares	96	168
	C	2½"	6	11	2½" squares	96	168
Dark green print	Vines	27" × 27"	1	—			
		30" × 30"	—	1			

Cutting Chart

strips and a rich green print for the corner squares. Add a narrow inner border of orchid batik, perhaps borrowed from one of the blocks. Finish with an elegant white-on-white outer border. White makes the perfect contrast to the appliqué floral motifs, which are cut from leftover scraps of fabric used elsewhere in the quilt.

To develop your color scheme, photocopy the **Color Plan** on page 75, and use colored pencils or crayons to experiment with different color arrangements.

CUTTING

All measurements include ¼-inch seam allowances. No templates are required for the pieces in these blocks, since every piece can be rotary cut. For easy reference, however, a letter identification is given for each pattern piece or unit in the **Block Diagram**.

Templates are used to cut pieces for the appliqué flowers and leaves. Make templates for appliqué pieces X, Y, and Z from the patterns on page 74. Refer to page 109 for complete information on making and using templates for appliqué.

Refer to the Cutting Charts and cut the required number of strips and pieces in the sizes needed. Cut all strips across the width of the fabric (crosswise grain). If you are working with scraps and do not have the full 42-inch width of fabric, be certain that your shorter strips total the full number of 42-inch strips required.

Note: We suggest that you cut and piece a sample block before cutting all of your fabric.

— Sew Easy

As you select the various fabrics for this quilt, keep in mind that a fabric may serve "double duty" by altering its position within the block. For example, a fabric used for the B triangle squares in one block might be used for the C perimeter squares in another.

Appliqué Cutting Chart

Fabric	Used For	Number to Cut Twin	Queen
Assorted medium and dark jewel-tone prints	Flowers (X)	48	60
Royal blue solid or print	Flower centers (Y)	48	60
Assorted green scraps	Leaves (Z)	88	112

ASSEMBLING THE BLOCK COMPONENTS

Refer to the Quilt Sizes chart to determine the required number of nine-patch units and triangle squares for the quilt you are making.

Piecing the Nine-Patch Units

The Sister's Choice block has a nine-patch unit (A) at its center. Each nine patch is made up of 2½-inch-wide strips cut from contrasting fabrics. The dark green floral strips remain consistent, but you'll want lots of combinations with the coordinating medium print strips. Before you begin to assemble the nine-patch units, you may wish to cut some of the strips into matching shorter lengths so that they can be mixed for greater variety.

Step 1. Sew a 2½-inch-wide dark green floral strip to each side of a 2½-inch-wide medium print strip to make a strip set, as shown in **Diagram 1**. Press the seams toward the green strips. This will be Strip Set 1.

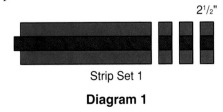

2½"

Strip Set 1

Diagram 1

Step 2. Square up one end of Strip Set 1, then cut it into 2½-inch segments, as shown.

Step 3. Sew a 2½-inch-wide strip of the same or a coordinating medium print to each side of a 2½-inch-wide green floral strip to make a strip set, as shown in **Diagram 2.** Press seam allowances toward the green strip. This will be Strip Set 2.

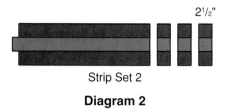

2½"

Strip Set 2

Diagram 2

Step 4. Square up one end of Strip Set 2, then cut it into 2½-inch segments.

Step 5. Continue making strip sets and cutting segments until you have made 48 Strip Set 1 segments for the twin-size or 84 segments for the queen-size quilt. Similarly, make 24 or 42 Strip Set 2 segments for the twin and queen, respectively.

Step 6. Matching seams carefully, sew identical Strip Set 1 segments to the top and bottom of a Strip Set 2 segment, as shown in **Diagram 3.** You may select a Strip Set 2 segment made with the same or a different print, depending on how scrappy you want your blocks. Place the segments in proper order, as shown, so the green floral is placed consistently in each unit. Press seam allowances away from the center segment.

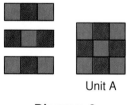

Unit A

Diagram 3

Step 7. Repeat to make the required number of nine-patch units for your quilt, as shown in the Quilt Sizes chart on page 67.

Piecing the Triangle-Square Units

We recommend that you use quick-piecing Method 2 on page 108 to make the triangle squares for this quilt. This method saves steps and is easy and accurate, while still allowing you to use a variety of fabrics for the triangle squares.

Refer to the Quilt Sizes chart and make the required number of triangle squares for your quilt using Method 2 on page 108. Pair four 2⅞-inch light floral squares with four identical 2⅞-inch jewel-tone squares to yield the eight identical triangle squares needed for each block.

PIECING THE SISTER'S CHOICE BLOCKS

Step 1. Select one nine-patch center (Unit A), eight identical triangle squares, four identical C squares, and four background D squares. Sew a triangle square to each side of a C square, as shown in **Diagram 4A.** Press seam allowances away from the triangle squares. Make four of these strips.

Step 2. Sew two of the strips to opposite sides of the nine patch, as shown in **4B..** Press seam allowances toward the nine patch.

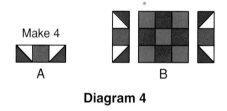

Make 4

A   B

Diagram 4

Step 3. Sew a background D square to each end of the remaining two strips, as shown in **Diagram 5A.** Press seam allowances toward the D squares.

Step 4. To complete the block, sew a strip to the top and bottom edges, as shown in **5B.** Press the block carefully.

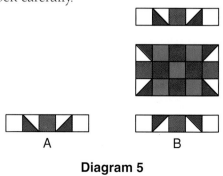

A   B

Diagram 5

Step 5. Repeat Steps 1 through 4 to assemble the required number of blocks for the size quilt you are making.

ASSEMBLING THE QUILT

Step 1. Use a design wall or other flat surface to arrange the blocks, sashing strips, and corner squares, as shown in the **Assembly Diagram.** The twin-size quilt has six horizontal rows of four blocks each. The queen-size quilt has seven horizontal rows of six blocks each.

Step 2. Sew the blocks, sashing strips, and corner squares in horizontal rows, as shown. Press all seams toward the blue sashing strips.

Step 3. Sew the rows together, matching seams carefully. Press the quilt.

ADDING THE MITERED BORDERS

This quilt has two mitered borders. The narrow batik and wide white border strips are sewn together first and are added to the quilt top as a single unit.

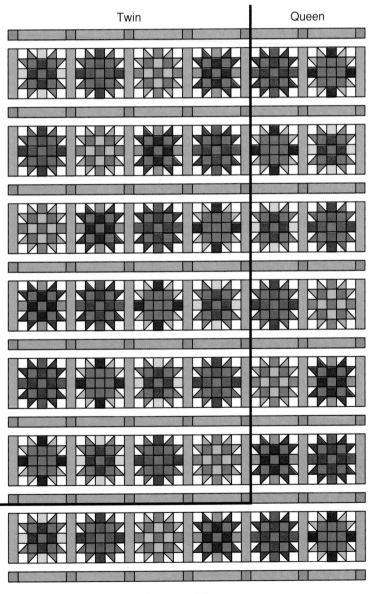

Twin   Queen

Assembly Diagram

Step 1. To determine the correct length for the side borders, measure the quilt top vertically through the center. To this measurement, add two times the finished width of both borders ($7\frac{1}{4} \times 2$ inches = $14\frac{1}{2}$ inches, plus 5 inches = $19\frac{1}{2}$ inches). This is the length you will need to make all the side border strips. In the same manner, measure the quilt top horizontally through the center, and calculate the lengths of the top and the bottom borders.

Step 2. Regardless of the size quilt you are making, you will need to sew some of the border strips together end to end to achieve the required length. For the twin-size quilt, fold two each of the batik and the white border strips into thirds. Trim off $\frac{1}{3}$ of each strip at the fold. Sew one full strip and a $\frac{1}{3}$ strip segment together for the top and the bottom borders. Sew one full strip and a remaining $\frac{2}{3}$ strip segment together for each of the side borders. Trim each of the border strips to the required lengths.

For the queen-size quilt, cut two each of the batik and the white border strips in half. For each border, sew two full strips and one half strip together, then trim to the required lengths.

Step 3. Beginning with the side border strips, pin and sew a batik and a white border strip together lengthwise to form a single side border unit. Press the seam toward the batik strip. Make two of these side border units. In the same manner, pin and sew the top and bottom border strips into units.

Step 4. Fold each border unit to find its midpoint, and crease. Sew the four border units to the appropriate sides of the quilt top, positioning the narrow batik border closest to the quilt top, as shown in the **Quilt Diagram** on the opposite page. Match and pin the midpoints and then follow the directions on page 119 for mitering borders.

PREPARING PIECES FOR APPLIQUÉ

Use your preferred method to prepare all flowers (X), flower centers (Y), and leaves (Z) for

appliqué. Refer to page 109 for information on an easy freezer paper method of appliqué.

MAKING THE VINES

Since they curve so gracefully, we recommend that you use bias strips to make the vines for the borders of your quilt. Refer to the instructions on page 110 in "Stars Basics" for information on preparing bias strips. For either quilt, cut the bias strips $1\frac{1}{8}$ inches wide. Then fold, press, and sew the strips as instructed. To avoid overlapping edges, sew strips together end to end to achieve the required lengths before folding and pressing. You will need approximately 360 inches of vine for the twin-size quilt, and 450 inches for the queen-size quilt.

·········Sew Quick·········

If you prefer to work with shorter lengths of bias vine, you can divide the single long piece into four shorter segments. For the twin-size quilt, you'll need approximately 75 inches of vine for both the top and the bottom borders and approximately 105 inches for each of the sides. For the queen-size quilt, you'll need approximately 105 inches for both the top and the bottom borders and approximately 120 inches for each of the sides. There's no need to worry about the raw edges where the segments meet—they'll be covered at each corner by an appliqué flower.

APPLIQUÉING THE OUTER BORDER

Step 1. Refer to the **Quilt Diagram** and position a prepared bias strip vine on each outer border, turning the corners as shown. Pin or baste the vines in place, then use your preferred method to appliqué the vine in place. Refer to "Choosing an Appliqué Method" on page 109 for more information.

Twin   Queen

Quilt Diagram

Step 2. Position flowers along the vine, as shown in the **Quilt Diagram.** For the twin-size quilt, place 9 flowers on the top and the bottom borders and 13 flowers on each side border. For the queen-size quilt, place 13 flowers on the top and bottom borders and 15 flowers on each side border. Center a flower over the intersection of

vines at each corner of the quilt. Pin or baste in place. Pin or baste a royal blue Y circle in the center of each flower. Use your preferred method to appliqué all flowers and flower centers.

Step 3. Position leaves along the vine as shown in the **Quilt Diagram**. For the twin-size quilt, place 18 leaves (in groups of two) on the top and bottom borders, and 26 leaves on each side border. For the queen-size quilt, place 26 leaves (in groups of two) on the top and bottom borders, and 30 leaves on each side border. Pin or baste the leaves in place, then appliqué using your preferred method. See "Choosing an Appliqué Method" on page 109.

QUILTING AND FINISHING

Step 1. Mark the top for quilting. The quilt shown has been machine quilted. An Orange Peel motif softens the angular lines of each pieced block. A continuous vine and leaf motif is quilted in the sashing strips. All of the flower and leaf appliqués are outlined, and the background of the white border is stipple quilted.

Step 2. Regardless of which quilt size you've chosen to make, the backing will need to be pieced. For the twin-size quilt, cut the backing fabric in half crosswise and trim the selvages. Cut two 18-inch-wide panels from the entire length of one piece. Sew a narrow panel to each side of the full-width piece, as shown in **Diagram 6.** The seams will run parallel to the sides of the quilt. Press the seams open.

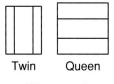

Twin   Queen

Diagram 6

For the queen-size quilt, divide the backing fabric crosswise into three equal pieces and trim the selvages. Cut a 33-inch-wide panel from the entire length of two of the pieces. Sew one of the narrower panels to each side of the full-width piece, as shown. The seams will run parallel to the top edge of the quilt. Press the seams open.

Step 3. Layer the backing, batting, and quilt top, and baste the layers together. Quilt by hand or machine, adding additional quilting of your choice as desired.

Step 4. Referring to the directions on page 121 in "Quiltmaking Basics," use the remaining royal blue fabric to make and attach double-fold binding to finish at a width of ¼ inch. To calculate the amount of binding you will need, add up the length of the four sides of the quilt plus 9 inches. The total is the approximate number of inches of binding you will need.

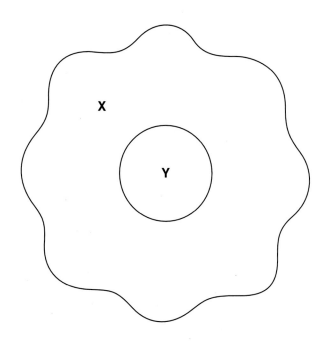

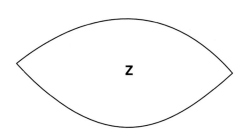

Sister's Choice
Color Plan

Photocopy this page and use it to experiment with color schemes for your quilt.

ORIGAMI STARS

Skill Level: *Easy*

*E*ast meets West in this star-studded beauty by Doris Krauss
Adomsky of Ivyland, Pennsylvania. She gives the classic Milky
Way a unique twist—literally!—with the addition of a folded, origami-
style center. Quick-cutting and easy-piecing methods make construction
a breeze, and the cool blue color scheme is a winner in any galaxy.

BEFORE YOU BEGIN

This quilt is based on the traditional Milky Way block. The center of each star is folded in the Japanese origami style, making the design truly three-dimensional.

Also, a clever combination of Star blocks and pieced connector strips creates the appearance of interlocking light and dark stars spinning through space.

While the three-dimensional nature of the design—and its accompanying weight—might make this project a bit impractical on a very large scale, it makes a terrific topper for a twin-size bed, especially when teamed with a tailored dust ruffle and pillow shams. And, of course, it is a knockout on the wall!

All pieces for this quilt are strips and shapes that can be rotary cut. To make construction even more simple and efficient, the four patch squares are strip pieced, and the multiple triangle squares are assembled using a quick-piecing grid method.

CHOOSING FABRICS

This quiltmaker has chosen blue as the dominant color for her dynamic five-fabric quilt.

Whether you select blue as your main color or prefer your own favorite color, remember that high contrast between the light and dark fabrics is especially important in the design of this quilt.

Quilt Sizes

	Wallhanging (shown)	Twin
Finished Quilt Size	38" × 38"	62" × 78"
Finished Star Block Size	6"	6"
Number of Star Blocks	16	63
Number of Four Patches	64	252
Number of Triangle Squares	112	472
Number of Light Folded Squares	24	110
Number of Dark Folded Squares	25	111
Number of Connector Strips	24	110

Materials

Fabric	Wallhanging (shown)	Twin
Multicolor print*	1¼ yards	2⅛ yards
Light blue print	1⅛ yards	3⅝ yards
Dark blue print	1 yard	2¾ yards
Red-violet print	⅓ yard	⅞ yard
Muslin	⅓ yard	1⅛ yards
Moss green print	¼ yard	⅓ yard
Backing	1¼ yards	4½ yards
Batting	45" × 45"	69" × 85"
Binding	⅓ yard	½ yard

NOTE: *Yardages are based on 44/45-inch-wide fabrics that are at least 42 inches wide after preshrinking.*

* *Assumes fabric is cut lengthwise, with four repeats across the width of the fabric.*

77

Cutting Chart

Fabric	Used For	Strip Width or Pieces	Number to Cut Wall	Number to Cut Twin	Second Cut Dimensions	Number to Cut Wall	Number to Cut Twin
Multicolor	Outer borders	3½"	4	7			
Dark blue	Folded squares	3½"	3	10	3½" squares	25	111
	Triangle squares	22" × 25"	1				
		42" × 42"	—	1			
		20" × 24"	—	1			
Light blue	Folded squares	3½"	2	10	3½" squares	24	110
	Triangle squares	22" × 25"	1				
		42" × 42"	—	1			
		20" × 24"	—	1			
	Four patches	1½"	5	18			
Red-violet	Four patches	1½"	5	18			
Moss green	Inner borders	1¼"	4	7			
Muslin	Folded square foundations	2½"	4	14	2½" squares	49	221

Look for fabrics that contrast sharply in value and also vary in visual texture (small-scale versus large-scale, subtle versus bold). This will allow the interlocking light and dark stars to emerge clearly when the blocks and connector strips are sewn together.

To develop your own color scheme for the quilt, photocopy the **Color Plan** on page 83, and use crayons or colored pencils to experiment with different color arrangements.

CUTTING

All measurements include ¼-inch seam allowances. No templates are required, as every piece is rotary cut. Refer to the Cutting Chart and cut the required number of strips and pieces in the sizes needed. With the exception of the border strip, cut all fabrics across the width of the fabric (on the crosswise grain).

Note: We recommend that you cut and piece one sample block before cutting all of the fabric for your quilt.

ASSEMBLING THE QUILT COMPONENTS

Each Star block in this quilt is composed of a dark folded (origami-style) square, four identical triangle-square units, and four identical four patch units. (See the **Block Diagram** for proper placement of four patches and triangle squares.) Connector strips join the blocks to give the quilt its overall appearance of light and dark interlocking stars.

Block Diagram

Each of these connector strips is composed of a light folded (origami-style) square and two identical triangle-square units, as shown in the **Connector Strip Diagram** on the opposite page.

Connector Strip Diagram

Making the Triangle Squares

Star points are created by triangle squares made from the dark blue and light blue prints, as shown in the **Block Diagram** on the opposite page. The grid method is the ideal choice to assemble the star points for this quilt, since it requires many *identical* triangle-square units (refer to Method 1 on page 107). For the wallhanging, pin the 22 × 25-inch dark and light blue fabrics with their right sides together, and mark a 7-square-wide and 8-square-tall grid of $2\frac{7}{8}$-inch squares on the lighter fabric. For the twin-size quilt, mark a 14-square-wide and 14-square-tall grid of $2\frac{7}{8}$-inch squares on the 42 × 42-inch square, and mark a 6-square-tall and 7-square-wide grid of $2\frac{7}{8}$-inch squares on the 20 × 24-inch rectangle. Sew, cut, and press to assemble the number of triangle squares required for your quilt, as shown in the Quilt Sizes chart.

·······Sew Quick·······

Before pressing the triangle-square units, stack the triangles with the dark fabric on top. Then, as you flip the dark triangle open to press, the seam allowance will automatically fall toward the darker piece.

Piecing the Four Patch Units

Step 1. Sew a $1\frac{1}{2}$-inch-wide light blue strip to a $1\frac{1}{2}$-inch-wide red-violet strip along its long edge, as shown in **Diagram 1**. Carefully press the seam toward the dark strip.

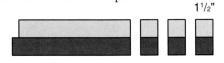

1½"

Diagram 1

Step 2. Square up one end of the strip set, then cut it into $1\frac{1}{2}$-inch segments. Remember to stop cutting and resquare your strip set often to make sure your four patch units will line up perfectly. Keep sewing strip sets and cutting them into segments until you have cut 128 segments for the wallhanging or 504 segments for the twin-size quilt.

Step 3. Sew two segments together, as shown in **Diagram 2**, matching the center seam carefully. Press. Repeat to assemble the number of four patch units required for your quilt, as shown in the Quilt Sizes chart.

Diagram 2

Making the Folded (Origami) Squares

Step 1. Place a $3\frac{1}{2}$-inch light or dark blue print square right side up on top of a $2\frac{1}{2}$-inch muslin square. Match and pin the corners of the print square to the corners of the muslin square. You should now see a fabric "bubble" at the center of the print square, as shown in **Diagram 3**.

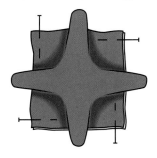

Diagram 3

Step 2. Fold the square sandwich in half, muslin-side in, aligning the edges. Finger press a 1-inch-long crease along one end of the fold, as shown in **Diagram 4A** on page 80, taking care not to extend the crease into the center of the square. Unfold the sandwich, right side up. Fold the excess of the top (print) fabric to the right and pin it in place, as shown in **4B** on page 80. Both squares should now measure $2\frac{1}{2}$ inches along the pinned edge.

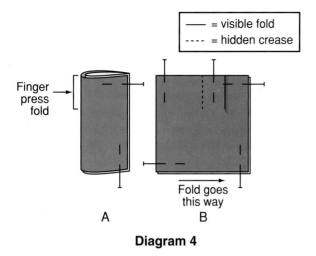

Diagram 4

Step 3. Turn the square clockwise and fold it in half again. Make another 1-inch-long crease, then unfold and pin in place, as shown in **Diagram 5A**. Make sure the new fold is also folded to the right. Repeat for the remaining two sides of the square, folding all creases in the same direction, as shown in **5B**. The excess fabric at the center should now resemble an on-point square, as shown.

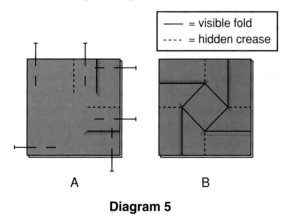

Diagram 5

Step 4. Press the square lightly and remove the corner pins (keep the creases pinned). The folds will be secured when the square is sewn into the block.

Step 5. Repeat Steps 1 through 3 to make the required number of light and dark folded squares for your quilt, as shown in the Quilt Sizes chart.

PIECING THE CONNECTOR STRIPS

Sew a triangle-square unit to each side of a light folded square, taking care to position the triangle

Sew Easy

It's fun to add a folded square or two (or dozens!) to any patchwork project. Simply substitute a folded square anywhere you would normally stitch a flat square. If you need larger or smaller folded squares than the 2-inch size featured in this project, use this handy formula to calculate the size squares you will need to cut:

Muslin: cut size needed for project (finished size + ½ inch for seam allowance).

Quilt fabric: cut 50 percent (or 1½ times) larger than the *finished size* of the muslin square + ½ inch for seam allowances.

For instance, if your project calls for 3-inch *finished* squares, cut your muslin squares 3½ inches. But the quilt fabric squares would need to be cut 5 inches (3 inches × 1½ = 4½ + ½ = 5 inches).

squares as shown in the **Connector Strip Diagram** (shown on page 79). Remove the pins holding the folds on the sewn sides of the square. Press the seams toward the center square. Repeat until you have made the required number of connector strips for your quilt, as shown in the Quilt Sizes chart on page 77.

PIECING THE STAR BLOCK

Step 1. Arrange a dark folded square and four each of the four patch units and the triangle squares in rows, as shown in **Diagram 6A** on the opposite page. Take care to position the triangle squares and the four patches correctly. Sew the units into rows, pressing the seams toward the triangle squares.

Step 2. Sew the rows together, as shown in **6B**. Remove all remaining pins in the folded squares. Press seams away from the center row.

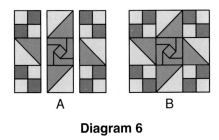

Diagram 6

Step 3. Repeat Steps 1 and 2 to make the total number of Star blocks required for your quilt. The extra dark, folded squares will become the corner squares for the connector strips. You should have the exact number of triangle squares for the wall-hanging, but a few extras (resulting from the grid-piecing method) for the twin-size quilt.

ASSEMBLING THE QUILT TOP

The **Assembly Diagram** illustrates the layout and the piecing process for several rows. Refer to the **Quilt Diagram** on page 82 for the complete layout of the twin-size and wall quilts. (The wall-hanging has four horizontal rows of four Star blocks each.) The blocks and rows are separated by connector strips.

Step 1. Arrange the Star blocks, connector strips, and dark folded squares in horizontal rows, as shown in the **Assembly** and **Quilt Diagrams.**

Assembly Diagram

Step 2. Sew the blocks, the connector strips, and the dark, folded squares into horizontal rows. Press the seams in adjacent rows in opposite directions.

Step 3. Sew the rows together, matching seams carefully. Remove all remaining pins from the dark, folded squares. Press the quilt.

ADDING THE BORDERS

The quilt shown features a double mitered border. You will need to sew the border strips together in pairs (green and multicolor print) for each side of the quilt before attaching them to the quilt top. The miters will then be completed in each corner as a unit.

Step 1. To calculate the length of the side borders, measure the quilt top through its vertical center and add 13 to this measurement. Repeat to calculate the length of the top and bottom borders, this time measuring the quilt through its horizontal center.

Step 2. Fold each side border in half to find its midpoint. Determine the midpoint for each side of the quilt.

Step 3. Pin and sew the green edges of the four border strips to the appropriate sides of the quilt top. Match and pin the midpoints, and then follow the directions on page 119 for mitering borders. Sew the miters, and press the quilt top.

QUILTING AND FINISHING

Step 1. The quilt shown is quilted in the ditch around the light and dark stars. Avoid quilting in the folded squares in order to maintain the three-dimensional effect.

Step 2. Piece the twin-size quilt backing (no piecing is necessary for the wallhanging). Cut the backing fabric in half crosswise; trim the selvages. Cut two 11-inch-wide panels from the entire length of one segment, and sew one to each side of the full-width piece, as shown in **Diagram 7** on page 82.

Wallhanging   Twin

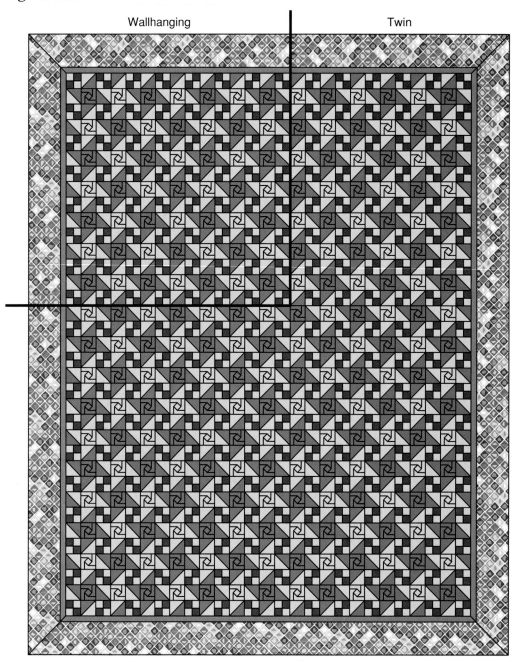

Quilt Diagram

The seams will run parallel to the sides of the quilt. Press the seams open.

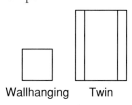

Wallhanging   Twin

Diagram 7

Step 3. Layer the backing, batting, and quilt top, and baste the layers together. Hand or machine quilt as desired.

Step 4. Referring to the directions on page 121 in "Quiltmaking Basics," make and attach double-fold binding to finish at ¼ inch wide. To calculate the total amount of binding you will need, add up the length of the four sides of the quilt plus 9 inches.

ORIGAMI STARS
Color Plan

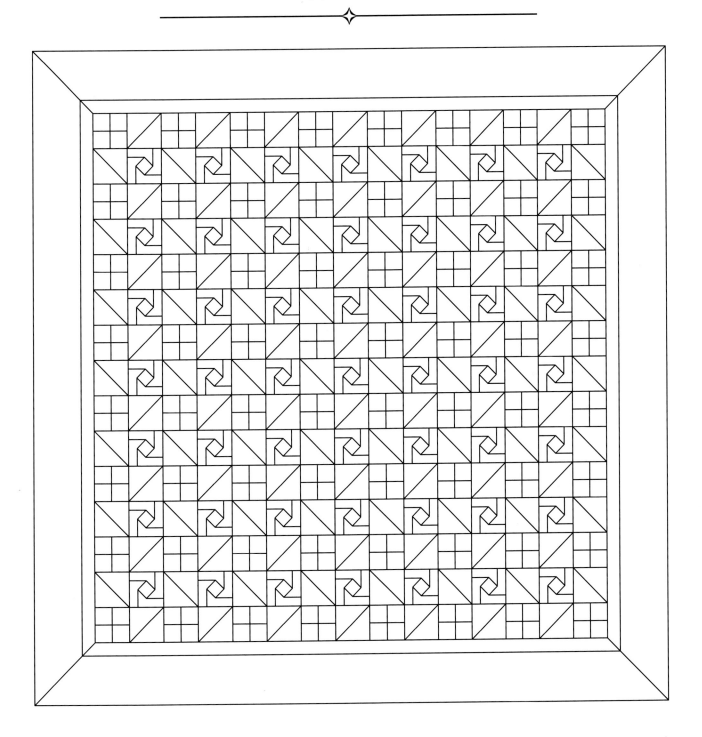

Photocopy this page and use it to experiment with color schemes for your quilt.

FEATHERED STAR

Skill Level: *Challenging*

*F*eathered Star quilts have been challenging quiltmakers for many generations. The dramatic red, black, and white version shown here, made early in the twentieth century, is an example of just such a quilt. The charm of this rustic beauty lies in the powerful color scheme and in the determination of the unknown quiltmaker to attempt this exciting pattern long before rotary cutters were available to make things easier and more accurate. The well-used, well-worn look of the quilt makes us certain it was well-loved by its owner.

BEFORE YOU BEGIN

The maker of this antique Feathered Star created a maverick of a quilt, for reasons unknown to us. Notice that one row of stars is incomplete and that only two sides are bordered. Our directions, however, are for making a quilt top with complete stars in each row, as shown in the **Assembly Diagram** on page 89. Since the pieced edges provide such a pleasing frame, the borders have been eliminated.

The directions are primarily for rotary cutting and quick piecing techniques; however, two templates are provided to eliminate dealing with "fussy" rotary measurements. You will also need to trace the printed grid to make the small triangle squares, as these finish at $1\frac{1}{16}$ inch, a measurement that isn't marked on rotary rulers.

Refer to "Stars Basics," beginning on page 104, and "Quiltmaking Basics," beginning on page 112, before starting this project. You'll find lots of information and tips on rotary cutting and grid piecing there.

Quilt Size

Finished Quilt Size	63" × 84"
Finished Block Size	21"
Number of Star Blocks	12

NOTE: Due to the complexity of the design, no size variations are provided.

Materials

Fabric	Amount
Red solid	$2\frac{5}{8}$ yards
Black solid	3 yards
White pindot	$2\frac{1}{8}$ yards
Backing	$5\frac{1}{8}$ yards
Batting	70" × 91"
Binding	$\frac{1}{2}$ yard

NOTE: Yardages are based on 44/45-inch-wide fabrics that are at least 42 inches wide after preshrinking.

CHOOSING FABRICS

This quilt contains only three fabrics. What makes the pattern so bold and graphic is the high degree of contrast among the fabrics used. Both the black and white are striking against the bold red of the emerging star pattern. You might easily find all three of these fabrics in quilt shops today, although any high-contrast, three-color combination would work as well.

To create your own color scheme for this project, photocopy the **Color Plan** on page 91, and use crayons or colored pencils to experiment with different color arrangements.

Cutting Chart

Fabric	Used For	Strip Width or Pieces	Number to Cut	Second Cut Dimensions	Number to Cut
Red solid	E	5⅜"	7	5⅜" squares	48
	F	7⅝"	3	7⅝" squares	12
	G	5"	6	5" squares	48
Black solid	Unit A	32" × 34"	1		
	Unit B	30" × 30"	1		
	C	Template C	48		
	I	9½"	3	9½" squares	12
White pindot	Unit A	32" × 34"	1		
	Unit B	30" × 30"	1		
	D	Template D	48		
	H	2"	3	2" squares	48

CUTTING

All measurements include ¼-inch seam allowances. Refer to the Cutting Chart and cut the required number of pieces and strips in the sizes needed. Cut all strips across the width of the fabric (crosswise grain). Make a template for piece C by tracing one square from the grid on page 90. This square will be subcut to make the "extra feather" triangles for each Star block. Make a template for piece D from the pattern on page 90. Refer to page 116 for complete details on making and using templates. Two sizes of triangle squares are used in this quilt, and both are pieced using the grid method, which requires sewing before cutting. See "Making the Triangle Squares" on the opposite page for additional instructions.

After you have cut the pieces listed above, you will need to make the following subcuts:

• Cut each 5⅜-inch red E square in half once diagonally.

• Cut each 7⅝-inch red F square in half *twice* diagonally.

• Cut the black C squares in half once diagonally.

Note: We suggest you cut and piece a sample block of each type of unit before cutting all of the fabric for your quilt.

Sew Easy

Cutting pattern pieces so that the straight of grain falls along the outer edge of a unit or block helps stabilize the block and minimize the stretching that occurs naturally when the block is handled. Advance planning is especially important when working with triangles, which *always* have at least one bias edge. When you are cutting the C squares for this quilt, lay the template on the fabric with the diagonal along the straight of grain, following the direction of the arrow. When the "extra feather" C triangles are cut from these squares, the diagonal edges will be on the straight of grain—perfect placement for this block!

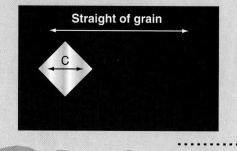

MAKING THE TRIANGLE SQUARES

Two sizes of triangle squares, shown in **Diagram 1**, are used in this quilt. Both sizes can be made quickly and accurately using the grid method of piecing. Refer to Method 1 on page 107, for instructions on assembling triangle squares.

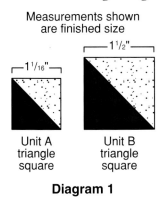

Measurements shown are finished size

Unit A triangle square

Unit B triangle square

Diagram 1

Step 1. You will need a total of 480 Unit A triangle squares, which have a finished size of $1\frac{1}{16}$ inches. Carefully trace the grid on page 90, duplicating it to draw a grid 15 squares across and 16 down on the reverse side of the 32 × 34-inch white pindot rectangle. Sew it to the matching black solid rectangle using the techniques described on page 107. Cut apart the triangle squares, as instructed.

Step 2. You will need a total of 288 Unit B triangle squares, which have a finished size of $1\frac{1}{2}$

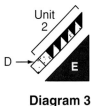

······ Sew Quick ········

Since the two triangle-square units for this quilt are so similar, it is especially important that they be kept separate. Label a large, self-sealing plastic storage bag for each of the two units. Place each batch of triangle squares into the appropriately labeled bag as soon as it is stitched, cut, and pressed. You'll not only save time, you'll also minimize the chance of a mix-up when it is time to begin assembling the blocks.

inches. Draw a $2\frac{3}{8}$-inch grid, 12 squares across and 12 squares down, on the reverse side of the 30-inch square of white pindot print. With right sides facing, sew it to the matching black solid square using the techniques described on page 107. Cut apart the triangle squares as instructed.

ASSEMBLING THE QUILT COMPONENTS

This quilt is assembled in units and rows, rather than in blocks. The stars are formed as the units and rows are joined.

Unit A

Step 1. Sew five A triangle squares into a rectangular unit, taking extra care to position them as shown in **Diagram 2A**. Sew a black C triangle to the left end of Unit 1, as shown in **2B**. Make a second rectangular unit by sewing five A triangle squares into a rectangle, this time taking care to position them as shown in **2C**. Sew a black C triangle to the right end of Unit 2, as shown in **2D**. Press the seam allowances toward the dark triangles in each of the units, trimming slightly if necessary to reduce bulk.

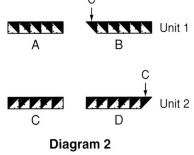

Diagram 2

Step 2. Sew a white D square to the left end of your finished Unit 2, as shown in **Diagram 3**. Press the seam allowance away from the white D square.

Diagram 3

Step 3. Sew Unit 2 to the longest side of a red E triangle, as shown in **Diagram 3** on page 87. Press the seam allowance toward the red triangle.

Step 4. Position a red F triangle as shown in **Diagram 4**, and sew Unit 1 to its short left side. Press the seam allowance toward the red triangle.

Diagram 4

Step 5. Sew the units assembled in Steps 3 and 4 together, as shown in **Diagram 5**. Be sure to carefully match the seam where the dark triangle meets the white square.

Diagram 5

Step 6. Complete Unit A by sewing another red E triangle to its lower left edge, as shown in **Diagram 6**. Press the seam allowance toward the red triangle.

Unit A

Diagram 6

Step 7. Repeat Steps 1 through 7 to make 48 of Unit A.

Unit B
Step 1. Sew three B triangle squares into a rectangular unit, as shown in **Diagram 7A.** Press the seams toward the dark triangles. Sew the rectangular unit to the bottom edge of a 5-inch red G

square, as shown in **7B**. Press the seam toward the triangle square unit.

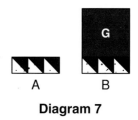

Diagram 7

Step 2. Sew three B triangle squares into a rectangular unit, adding a 2-inch white H square to its end, as shown in **Diagram 8A**. Press the seam allowances toward the dark triangles to avoid show-through, if possible. Sew this strip to the right edge of the unit assembled in Step 1, as shown in **8B**, taking care to match intersecting seams. Press.

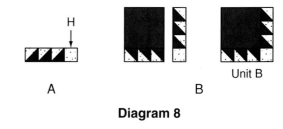

Diagram 8

Step 3. Repeat Steps 1 and 2 to make 48 of Unit B.

ASSEMBLING THE QUILT TOP
Before the quilt top can be assembled, some of the A and B Units must be assembled into larger blocks. Refer to the **Assembly Diagram** on the opposite page as needed.

Step 1. Sew two B units together, as shown in **Diagram 9**. Press. Repeat, assembling a total of 10 identical rectangles. These will be used around the outer edges of the quilt.

Diagram 9

Step 2. Sew together two B units as in Step 1. Repeat, assembling another unit. Press adjoining seams in opposite directions, and sew the two units together, as shown in **Diagram 10.** Press. Assemble a total of six identical square blocks to be used in rows 3, 5, and 7 of the quilt.

Step 3. Sew two A units together, as shown in **Diagram 11.** Press. Assemble a total of 17 identical rectangular blocks to be used horizontally in rows 2, 4, 6, and 8, and vertically in rows 3, 5, and 7.

Diagram 11

Diagram 10

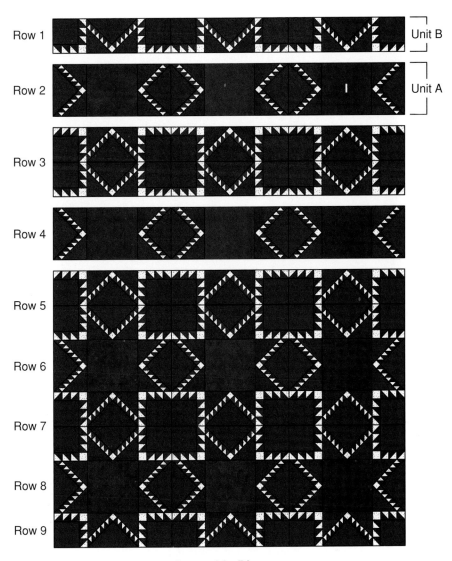

Assembly Diagram

Step 4. Use a design wall to arrange all pieced segments and the 9½-inch black squares (I) into nine rows, as shown in the **Assembly Diagram** on page 89. Note that the remaining A and B units are used around the outer edges of the quilt.

Step 5. Sew the components of each row together. Press seams in adjoining rows in opposite directions where possible. Sew the rows together, matching all seam intersections. Press the quilt top.

QUILTING AND FINISHING

Step 1. Mark the top for quilting. The quilt on page 84 is quilted in an overall Baptist Fan motif.

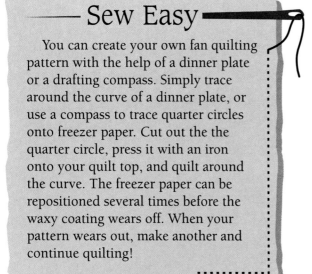

— Sew Easy

You can create your own fan quilting pattern with the help of a dinner plate or a drafting compass. Simply trace around the curve of a dinner plate, or use a compass to trace quarter circles onto freezer paper. Cut out the the quarter circle, press it with an iron onto your quilt top, and quilt around the curve. The freezer paper can be repositioned several times before the waxy coating wears off. When your pattern wears out, make another and continue quilting!

Step 2. To make the backing, cut the backing fabric in half across the width of the fabric, and trim the selvages. Cut two 15-inch-wide panels from the entire length of one segment, then sew a narrow panel to each side of the full-width piece, as shown in **Diagram 12**. The seams will run parallel to the sides of the quilt. Press the seams open.

Diagram 12

Step 3. Layer the backing, batting, and quilt top. Baste the layers together. Hand or machine quilt, adding additional quilting as desired.

Step 4. Referring to the directions on page 121, make and attach double-fold binding to finish at a width of ¼ inch. To calculate the amount of binding you will need for your quilt, add the length of the four sides of the quilt plus 9 inches.

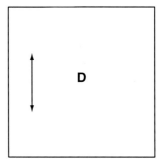

D

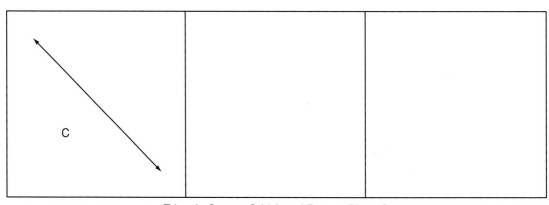

C

Triangle Square Grid A and Pattern Piece C
(seam allowances included)

FEATHERED STAR

Color Plan

Photocopy this page and use it to experiment with color schemes for your quilt.

SOLITUDE

Skill Level: *Intermediate*

*J*ohanna Wilson's expert piecing and Bonnie Erikson's spectacular feathered machine quilting make this wallhanging a real knockout. Johanna chose just two fabrics, but unlike many quilts made from a pair of fabrics, this one packs a colorful punch. The paisley print used is rich with burgundies, greens, teals, golds, and browns, providing a range of strong colors. Solitude is just one of over two dozen quilts Johanna has designed using the traditional Fox and Geese block in original settings.

BEFORE YOU BEGIN

This quilt is constructed using rotary cutting techniques and your choice of quick-piecing methods.

Each 12-inch star block is actually made up of four 6-inch Fox and Geese blocks. To form the intricate-looking diagonal setting, the 12-inch blocks are separated by plain setting squares, and pairs of 6-inch blocks are placed near the outer edges of the quilt corners.

CHOOSING FABRICS

The original quilt contains only two fabrics. A medium tan print is used for setting squares and rectangles and all background areas of the blocks. For a blended, consistent background, choose a very small print or one that "reads" as a solid. For example, the print you choose may appear to be solid at first glance, but when examined more closely, you find it is actually an overall print or pattern. A print of this type will add more texture to

your quilt than a true solid.

For the star points, choose a medium-scale print. The print can be multicolor, as in the quilt shown, but be sure that all colors in the print contrast with the background fabric that you have chosen so the star points are

clearly distinguishable from the background fabric.

To develop your own color scheme, photocopy the **Color Plan** on page 97, and use colored pencils or crayons to experiment with different color arrangements.

Quilt Sizes

	Wallhanging (shown)	King
Finished Quilt Size	54½" × 54½"	102½" × 102½"
Finished Block Size	6"	6"
Number of Blocks	32	128
Number of 3" Triangle Squares	72	280
Number of 1½" Triangle Squares	128	512

Materials

Fabric	Wallhanging	King
Tan print	4 yards	11⅞ yards
Teal print*	2 yards	5 yards
Backing	3½ yards	9⅓ yards
Batting	62" × 62"	110" × 110"

NOTE: *Yardages are based on 44/45-inch-wide fabrics that are at least 42 inches wide after preshrinking.*

* *Yardages include binding.*

Cutting Chart

Fabric	Used For	Strip Width	Number to Cut Wall	Number to Cut King	Second Cut Dimensions	Number to Cut Wall	Number to Cut King
Tan	Setting squares	12½"	2	8	12½" squares	4	24
	Setting rectangles	6½"	3	6	12½" × 6½"	8	16
	Border rectangles	21½"	1	1	21½" × 3½"*	8	8
	Border rectangles	18½"	—	1	18½" × 3½"	—	8
	Large triangle squares	25"	1	4	25" squares	1	4
	Small triangle squares	20"	1	2	20" squares	1	4
	Pieced blocks	2"	7	26	2" squares	128	512
Teal	Large triangle squares	25"	1	4	25" squares	1	4
	Small triangle squares	20"	1	2	20" squares	1	4
	Border corners	3½"	1	1	3½" squares	4	4

* Cut these pieces on the lengthwise grain.

CUTTING

Refer to the Cutting Chart for the number of pieces to cut from each fabric for your quilt size. All measurements include ¼-inch seam allowances.

Note: Cut and piece one sample block before cutting all of the fabric for the quilt.

MAKING THE TRIANGLE SQUARES

Two sizes of triangle squares are used in this quilt. Each Fox and Geese block contains four 1½-inch triangle squares and two 3-inch triangle squares (finished sizes). The 3-inch triangle squares are also used in the border.

Triangle squares can be made quickly and accurately using the grid method, which is described on page 107.

Step 1. For the 1½-inch triangle squares, use a 2⅜-inch grid with eight squares across and eight squares down. Make one grid for the wallhanging or four grids for the king-size quilt.

Step 2. Use a 3⅞-inch grid with six squares across and six squares down for the 3-inch triangle squares. Make one grid for the wallhanging or four grids for the king-size quilt.

MAKING THE FOX AND GEESE BLOCKS

Step 1. Sew a 2-inch square to a small triangle square, as shown in **Diagram 1A**. Press toward the dark triangle. Repeat to make four units. Sew the units together in pairs, as shown in **1B**. Press.

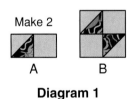

Make 2

A   B

Diagram 1

Step 2. Sew a large triangle square to one end of each bow-tie unit, positioning the units as shown in **Diagram 2A**. Press toward the large dark triangles. Sew together, as shown in **2B**. Press.

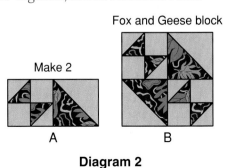

Fox and Geese block

Make 2

A   B

Diagram 2

Diagram 5

Step 3. Repeat Steps 1 and 2 to complete the number of Fox and Geese blocks needed for your quilt size. The remaining large triangle squares will be used in the border.

ASSEMBLING THE STAR BLOCKS

Step 1. Position and sew two Fox and Geese blocks together, as shown in **Diagram 3**. Repeat, sewing all but four Fox and Geese blocks into pairs. Set the remaining four blocks aside to be used in the quilt corners.

Diagram 3

Step 2. Sew two units from Step 1 together to create a Star block, orienting them as shown in **Diagram 4**. Match the seams carefully, and press the adjoining seams in opposite directions where possible.

Star Block

Diagram 4

Step 3. Repeat, assembling 5 Star blocks for the wallhanging and 25 for the king-size quilt. The remaining Fox and Geese block pairs will be used in the border.

Step 4. Sew the leftover large triangle squares together in pairs, as shown in **Diagram 5**. These will be used in the border.

ASSEMBLING THE QUILT TOP

Step 1. Refer to the photograph of the wallhanging or the **King-Size Assembly Diagram** on page 96, and use a design wall or other flat surface to lay out the Star blocks, setting pieces, and Fox and Geese blocks in horizontal rows.

Step 2. Sew the blocks and the setting squares and rectangles together in rows, pressing the seams toward the setting pieces. Sew the rows together, matching seam intersections carefully. Press the entire quilt top.

Step 3. Lay out the border rectangles, the remaining 3-inch triangle squares, and the border corners around the perimeter of the quilt. For the king-size quilt, use the larger rectangles at the corners and the smaller rectangles for the middle area of the border.

Step 4. Sew the top and bottom borders together in horizontal rows. Sew these borders to the quilt top, carefully matching seams and being sure the dark portion of the triangle squares is adjacent to the quilt top.

Step 5. Sew the side borders together in the same manner as the top and bottom borders, and sew one to each side of the quilt top.

QUILTING AND FINISHING

Step 1. Mark the top for quilting. In the quilt shown on page 92, feathered wreaths were used in the center of each setting square, feathered curves in each setting triangle, and feathered ropes in each border rectangle. To highlight the feathered quilting, the remaining background areas were stipple quilted. The dark star points were quilted in the ditch.

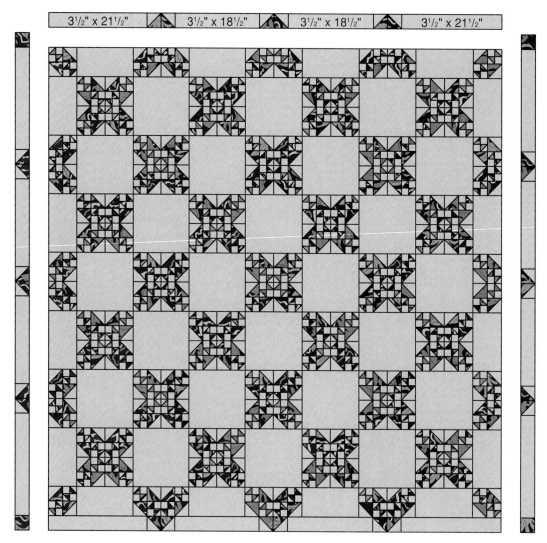

3½" x 21½"   3½" x 18½"   3½" x 18½"   3½" x 21½"

King-Size Assembly Diagram

Step 2. Regardless of which quilt size you're making, the backing will have to be pieced. For the wallhanging, cut the backing fabric in half crosswise and trim the selvages. Cut two 11-inch-wide pieces from the entire length of one segment. Sew one narrow piece to each side of the full-width piece, as shown in **Diagram 6.** Press the seams open.

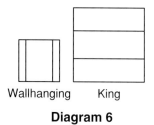

Wallhanging   King

Diagram 6

For the king-size quilt, cut the backing fabric into three equal lengths and trim the selvages. Cut a 35-inch-wide panel from the entire length of two of the segments and sew one to each side of the full-width piece, as shown. Press the seams open.

Step 3. Layer the backing, batting, and quilt top. Baste the layers together, then hand or machine quilt as desired.

Step 4. Referring to the directions on page 121, make and attach double-fold binding from the teal fabric. To calculate the amount of binding you will need, add up the length of the four sides of the quilt plus 9 inches.

SOLITUDE

Color Plan

Photocopy this page and use it to experiment with color schemes for your quilt.

MIDNIGHT IN PARADISE

Skill Level: *Easy*

*A*t last...the perfect cure for the coldest winter nights! A sizzling jungle print and bright, sun-splashed colors send Susan Stein's clever Evening Star adaptation straight to the tropical zone. With its efficient cutting and simple piecing, you'll be dreaming "under the stars" in no time!

———————————✦———————————

BEFORE YOU BEGIN

The directions for this quilt are written based on a variety of quick-cutting techniques. All of the pieces are strips and squares that can be rotary cut, and triangles are cut by subdividing squares. Fabrics can be layered for even more efficient cutting.

You may wish to read "Stars Basics," beginning on page 104, and "Quiltmaking Basics," beginning on page 112, before you begin this quilt. You'll find lots of helpful hints, tips, and techniques, in addition to specific instructions concerning the use of the rotary cutter.

CHOOSING FABRICS

The appeal of this cheerful quilt lies largely in its adventurous combination of fabrics. Begin by selecting a large-scale, multicolor tropical print, preferably with a black background. This key fabric will be used for the star centers and the outer border, and will establish the colorful, sun-washed flavor of your quilt. Choose a print with a bold mix of reds, oranges, lime greens, and sunny yellows. Or, as an alternative, opt

Quilt Sizes		
	Twin (shown)	King
Finished Quilt Size	59" × 83"	95" × 95"
Finished Block Size	12"	12"
Number of Blocks	24	49

Materials		
Fabric	Twin	King
Assorted bright solids and prints (*total*)	2⅛ yards	4¼ yards
Tropical print	1⅝ yards	2⅞ yards
Black solid	1½ yards	2¾ yards
Backing	5 yards	9 yards
Batting	66" × 90"	102" × 102"
Binding	½ yard	⅝ yard

NOTE: *Yardages are based on 44/45-inch-wide fabrics that are at least 42 inches wide after preshrinking.*

for a cooler blend of teals, hot pinks, and rich purples.

For the star backgrounds, select an array of subtle prints or solids in bright colors that complement the tropical print. These can be a wide variety of different fabrics, or you might select a few fabrics that grade from color to color or value to value on a single width of fabric.

All star points are cut from a single black solid. This provides the perfect counterpart to all the dazzling color and adds a touch of drama as well.

To develop your own color scheme for the quilt, photocopy the **Color Plan** on page 103, and use crayons or colored pencils to experiment with different color arrangements.

99

Cutting Chart

Fabric	Used For	Strip Width	Number to Cut Twin	Number to Cut King	Second Cut Dimensions	Number to Cut Twin	Number to Cut King
Assorted bright solids and prints	A	3⅞"	10	20	3⅞" squares	96	196
	C	3½"	8	17	3½" squares	96	196
Tropical print	Outer border	4½"	7	9			
	B	6½"	4	9	6½" squares	24	49
Black solid	Inner border	2"	8	9			
	A	3⅞"	10	20	3⅞" squares	96	196

CUTTING

All measurements include ¼-inch seam allowances. Refer to the Cutting Chart and cut the required number of pieces and strips in the sizes needed. Cut all strips across the width of the fabric (crosswise grain). For easy reference, a letter is given for each pattern piece in the **Block Diagram.**

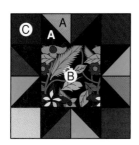

Block Diagram

You will cut some squares into triangles. For the star point and background triangles (piece A), cut the 3⅞-inch black and bright squares in half diagonally. You'll need the same number of black and brightly colored triangles: 192 for the twin and 392 for the king-size.

Note: Cut and piece a sample block before cutting all the fabric for your quilt.

PIECING THE STAR BLOCKS

Step 1. The backgrounds of the Star blocks are a scrappy mix. Sew a black A triangle to a random, brightly colored A triangle, as shown in **Diagram 1**. Press the seam toward the black triangle. Make eight triangle squares for each block, and clip off the triangle "ears."

Diagram 1

Step 2. Sew two triangle squares together to make Unit 1, as shown in **Diagram 2**. Make four of these units for each block and label them. Press the seam to one side.

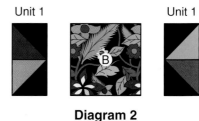

Diagram 2

Step 3. Sew a Unit 1 to the sides of a tropical print B square, as shown in **Diagram 2**. Press the seams toward the square.

Step 4. Sew a bright C square to each end of the remaining Unit 1 segments, as shown in **Diagram 3A** on the opposite page. Press the seams toward the squares. Sew strips to the top and bottom of the block, as shown in **3B**. *Do not press the block yet.*

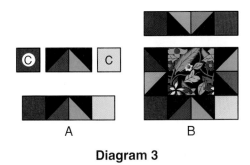

Diagram 3

Step 5. Repeat Steps 1 through 4 to assemble the total number of blocks required for your quilt.

ASSEMBLING THE QUILT TOP

Step 1. Arrange the blocks as shown in the **Quilt Diagram** on page 102. The twin-size quilt has six rows of four blocks each. The king-size quilt has seven rows of seven blocks each.

Step 2. Sew the blocks together into rows. Press seams within the blocks. When possible, press seams in adjoining rows in opposite directions. Sew rows together, matching all intersections. Press the quilt top.

ADDING THE BLACK INNER BORDER

Step 1. Measure the length of the quilt top through the center of the quilt. Sew two 2-inch-wide black strips end to end, press the seam, and trim to that measurement. Make two side border strips.

Step 2. Fold one border strip in half crosswise and crease. Unfold it and position it right side down along one side of the quilt, with its crease at the quilt's horizontal midpoint. Pin at the midpoint and ends first, then along the length of the entire side, easing in fullness if necessary. Sew the border to the quilt, and press seams toward the border. Repeat on the opposite side of the quilt.

Step 3. Measure the width of the quilt top through the center of the quilt. For the twin-size quilt, divide one of the remaining 2-inch-wide

border strips in half, and sew one half to each of the remaining two strips. Press the seam and trim to the measurement you have just taken. For the king-size quilt, follow the procedure described in Step 1 for piecing, pressing, and trimming.

Step 4. Repeat the process described in Step 2 to add the top and bottom borders to the quilt.

ADDING THE OUTER PRINT BORDER

Step 1. Determine the measurements for the outer side, top, and bottom borders in the same manner as described in Steps 1 and 3 of "Adding the Black Inner Border."

Step 2. Piece the borders for the twin- and king-size quilts in the same manner as described in Steps 1 and 3 of "Adding the Black Inner Border." For the king-size quilt, divide the remaining 4½-inch-wide border strip into four equal segments. Sew one of these short segments to each border strip to make the quilt's four outer borders. Press the seams as desired and trim to the appropriate measurements.

Step 3. Repeat Steps 2 and 4 of "Adding the Black Inner Border" to add the side, top, and bottom outer borders. Press the quilt.

QUILTING AND FINISHING

Step 1. Mark the top for quilting. The quilt shown is machine quilted in an overall diagonal grid, using the diagonal divisions in the half-square triangles as a guide, and with lines extending into the adjacent squares.

Step 2. The backing will need to be pieced. **Diagram 4** illustrates the layout for both quilt backs.

Diagram 4

For the twin-size quilt, cut the backing fabric in half crosswise and trim the selvages. Cut two 12-inch-wide panels from the entire length of one piece of backing fabric. Sew a narrow panel to each side of the full-width piece, as shown on page 101. Press the seams open.

For the king-size quilt, divide the entire length of backing fabric crosswise into three equal pieces, and trim the selvages. Cut a 29-inch-wide panel from the entire length of two of the pieces. Sew a narrow panel to each side of the full-width piece. Press the seams open.

Step 3. Layer the backing, batting, and quilt top, and baste together. Quilt as desired.

Step 4. Referring to the directions on page 121, make and attach double-fold binding to finish at a width of $1/4$ inch. To calculate the total amount of binding you will need, add up the length of the four sides of the quilt plus 9 inches.

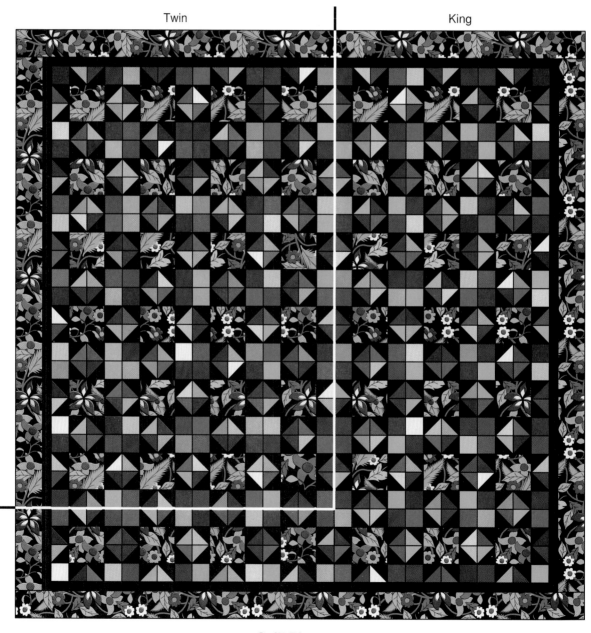

Quilt Diagram

MIDNIGHT IN PARADISE
Color Plan

Photocopy this page and use it to experiment with color schemes for your quilt.

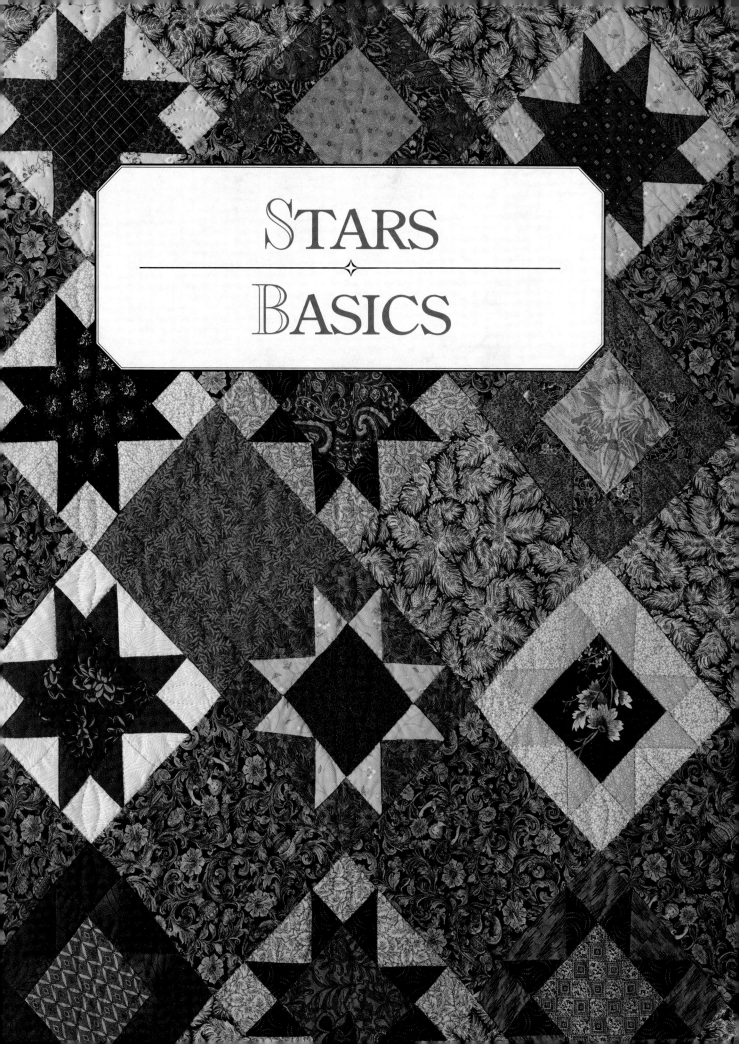

STARS

BASICS

USING STARS BASICS

The star motif is one of the most popular and versatile patterns in quiltmaking. In this section, you'll learn quick-and-easy techniques for cutting, piecing, and appliqué to help you with the many different star variations found in this book. It's a good idea to read through this section before beginning any of the projects.

WHAT IS VALUE?

When we speak of *value* in terms of quiltmaking, we refer to the relative lightness or darkness of color in fabrics. It is important to include fabrics of different values—lights, mediums, and darks—to create contrast within the design. It is this difference in value between the elements in a block or quilt top that allows us to see the pattern emerge. Color, in fact, is secondary to value.

It is possible to create a variety of effects depending upon how you place the light, medium, and dark fabrics within a quilt block. **Diagram 1** gives a clear example of how pattern is determined not only by contrast in value, but also by how the lights, mediums, and darks are positioned.

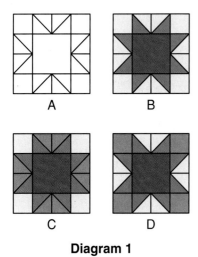

Diagram 1

All of the blocks are made up of the same arrangement of squares and triangles, as shown in **1A**. In **1B**, all of the background pieces are light, while all of the star points are dark. This contrast makes the star motif very obvious. In **1C**, the

background triangles are very similar in value to the star points, so the overall effect is less of a star and more of a cross. In **1D**, the corner blocks are very similar in value to the star points. Again, the image of the star becomes less obvious, but this time the image becomes more of an X, emphasizing the diagonal line of the block.

By studying these examples, it becomes obvious that the quiltmaker can control what the viewer sees simply by manipulating the placement of value within the design. Sometimes it is fun to include a variety of *different* value arrangements in

Sew Easy

As you are sorting fabrics into lights, mediums, and darks, you may find that color incorrectly influences your perception of value. Here are several ways to solve this problem:

• View your fabrics through a value filter. These inexpensive red plastic filters mask color, so the fabrics appear in shades of gray to black (similar to a black and white photograph). Value filters are available at quilt shops and through mail-order sources.

Note: Red often appears lighter than it really is through these filters, so be sure to evaluate reds in other ways, too.

• View fabrics from a distance. Do they blend together, or do a few pop out?

• Try viewing the fabrics through a reducing glass, available at many hardware stores and quilt shops.

• If you wear glasses, remove them. If not, try squinting at your fabrics. This will help to blur the lines between the individual fabrics, enabling you to determine if they are all fairly similar in value.

• Glue or pin swatches of fabrics side by side on a piece of paper, and make a black and white photocopy of it.

the blocks of a single quilt. This is especially true in scrap quilts, where this "visual surprise" adds interest and old-time charm.

You'll notice that a key word in the definition of value is *relative*. The lightness or darkness of a fabric is entirely dependent on the other fabrics around it. For example, a medium blue fabric looks dark when positioned against a pastel, but it becomes a light or medium when positioned next to black.

Before you begin each project, it might be helpful to review the values of the various fabrics you have selected. Begin with a quick sort, stacking fabrics in piles according to your first impression of their values. Then go back and take a closer look at the contents of each pile. Place the fabrics side by side, and view the group as a whole. If any fabric is noticeably lighter or darker than others in the group, remove it and consider using it with another group. Add and subtract fabrics until you have a good assortment for that particular value. Repeat the process for the remaining value groups.

The project directions in this book include general recommendations regarding value. This does not mean that all darks must be forest green, burgundy, black, or navy. Nor does it mean that all lights must be pale pastels. You can alter the overall appearance of the quilt by changing the range of values in general or by rearranging the placement of values within the design.

WORKING WITH WINDOW TEMPLATES

Sometimes it is helpful when piecing a block to have cut pieces that include not only exact ¼-inch seam allowances, but also clearly marked sewing lines. For example, a number of the projects in this book include blocks or units with set-in seams, a piecing technique that requires precise stops, starts, and pivoting. A window template allows you to mark both seam and cutting lines, making set-in seams a snap.

To make a window template, transfer both the solid cutting and the dashed seam lines of the pattern piece onto durable template plastic. It is important to use sturdy template material, espe-

cially when the window template will be reused many times. Use a sharp blade to cut out the shape on both the inner, dashed seam line and the outer, solid cutting line.

When you place the template on fabric, carefully trace both the inner and outer edges, as shown in **Diagram 2**. The inside edge of the window indicates the seam line and is the finished size of the piece. The outside edge of the template is the cut size, and includes the ¼-inch seam allowance.

Diagram 2

Once the template has been traced onto the fabric, the pieces can be rotary cut. Just be certain to cut on the outer—or cutting—line of the pieces.

MAKING TRIANGLE SQUARES

Many of the blocks in this book require multiple triangle-square units. A triangle square is made from two right triangles joined along their long sides, as shown in **Diagram 3**. The quick-cutting and quick-piecing techniques described here allow you to assemble large numbers of accurate units—and blocks—much more efficiently than is possible using more traditional methods.

Diagram 3

Method 1: The Grid Method

This method is a good choice when you need many *identical* triangle-square units. Two pieces of fabric are cut oversize, placed with their right sides together, then marked, sewn, and cut apart into individual triangle squares. Careful marking and sewing are musts, but your attention to detail will produce multiples of accurate, identical triangle squares, even in the tiniest of sizes. And you won't have to fuss with stretchy bias edges!

Step 1. To determine the correct size to cut the fabric, you must know the size of the squares in the grid and the number of squares you wish to make. This information is given in the directions for each project. The size of the squares is equal to the finished side of the triangle-square unit, plus $\frac{7}{8}$ inch. Each square in the grid will result in two triangle squares. In **Diagram 4,** the size of the squares in the grid is $3\frac{3}{8}$ inches and 60 triangles are required, so we need to draw a grid of 30 squares.

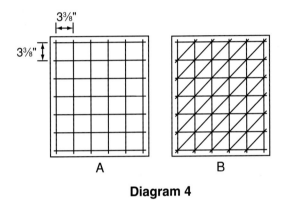

Diagram 4

A grid of five squares by six squares will yield a 30-square grid and requires a $17\frac{1}{2} \times 21$-inch piece of fabric. Since it's best to allow a little extra room on all sides of the grid, we would suggest that the two pieces be cut 22×25 inches.

Step 2. Working on the wrong side of the lighter fabric, use a pencil to draw a grid of squares, as shown in **Diagram 4A.** Draw the grid at least $\frac{1}{2}$ inch from the raw edges of the fabric. Referring to **4B,** carefully draw a diagonal line through each square in the grid.

Step 3. Position the marked fabric right sides together with the second piece of fabric. Pin the fabrics together, using one pin in every other square. Using a $\frac{1}{4}$-inch seam allowance, stitch along both sides of the diagonal lines, as shown in **Diagram 5.** Use the edge of your presser foot as a $\frac{1}{4}$-inch guide, or draw a light pencil line $\frac{1}{4}$ inch from each side of the diagonal line.

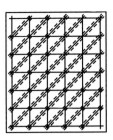

Diagram 5

Step 4. Use a rotary cutter and ruler to cut the grid apart. Cut on all of the solid marked lines, as indicated in **Diagram 6A.** Carefully press the triangle squares open, pressing each seam toward the darker fabric. (You may have to tug out a few stitches on the point opposite the seam.) Trim off the triangle points at the seam ends, as shown in **6B.** Continue marking and cutting triangle squares until you have made the number required.

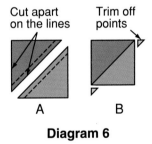

Diagram 6

········Sew Quick········

When stitching with the grid method, it is not necessary to break the stitching at the end of each diagonal line. Just raise the needle and lift the presser foot, rotate the fabric grid, and start stitching in the opposite direction.

Method 2: Triangle Squares from Squares
Another way to eliminate handling bias edges when making triangle squares is to cut squares,

sew them together diagonally, then cut them apart to yield two triangle squares. This method is useful for larger squares, or for when you need scrappy squares stitched from a wide assortment of fabrics.

Step 1. Determine the size square required by adding ⅞ inch to the desired finished size of the triangle square. Cut two squares to this size (or slightly larger). The resulting triangle squares can be trimmed to the finished size. The extra trimming step adds a bit more work, but it improves the accuracy of the finished block.

Step 2. Draw a diagonal line from corner to corner on the wrong side of the lighter square, as shown in **Diagram 7A.**

Step 3. Place two squares right sides together, matching the edges carefully. Sew ¼ inch from each side of the drawn line, as shown in **7B.** After sewing on both sides of the line, cut the squares in half on the diagonal lie, as shown in **7C.** Press the seam allowance in each unit toward the darkest fabric. Trim off tips from the triangle points.

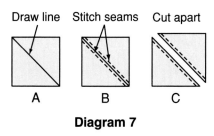

Diagram 7

CHOOSING AN APPLIQUÉ METHOD

A few of the projects in this book include appliqué. See page 117 in "Quiltmaking Basics" for general information on appliqué, as well as a description of the needle-turn technique.

In this section, we include a number of additional techniques to assist you with the specific projects in this book. You may find that a combination of methods will work best within the same quilt, depending on the individual shapes involved. We suggest that you experiment with each of these techniques to see which best suits your sewing style.

FREEZER PAPER APPLIQUÉ

Freezer paper can help make many appliqué projects easier. The paper acts as a stabilizer, allowing crisper points and smoother curves.

You can purchase plain white freezer paper at most grocery stores. Gridded freezer paper is available at many quilt shops.

Two different methods of freezer paper appliqué are explained here. Read through the directions for both, then choose the method that suits you best.

Method 1: Freezer Paper Appliqué
Step 1. Use a template to draw your patterns onto the dull (nonwaxy) side of the freezer paper.

Step 2. Cut out the shapes on the lines. Do not add a seam allowance.

——— Sew Easy ———

Here are a few extra pointers for needle-turn appliqué, which is described on page 118. Some of these tips may help with the other methods of appliqué described here as well.

• For a neater finished edge, clip inner points and curves before sewing. Make a perpendicular cut into an inner point, almost to the turn line. Make small V-shaped cuts on inner curves, again almost to the turn line. Make as many cuts as necessary to help you achieve a smooth fold. Take a few extra appliqué stitches at cuts to reinforce fabric. Use a drop of Fray Check as necessary to prevent raveling.

• Turn under points by cutting off the tip slightly. Fold the remaining seam allowance under to the turn line. Next, turn the seam allowance on one side of the point, then the other. To achieve a sharp point, it may be necessary to trim excess fabric at the folds as you work.

Step 3. Use a medium to hot, *dry* iron to press the shiny (waxy) side of the shapes onto the right side of your fabric, as shown in **Diagram 8**. The iron will adhere the paper to the fabric.

Diagram 8

Step 4. Cut out the shape from fabric, adding a ³/₁₆- to ¹/₄-inch seam allowance around all edges of the paper template, as shown in **Diagram 9**.

Diagram 9

Step 5. Peel away the freezer paper and center it, waxy side up, on the reverse side of your fabric. Press the seam allowance over the template, as shown in **Diagram 10**. The waxy coating will soften and hold your seam in place. This method eliminates basting, but you will still need to clip the curves and points.

Diagram 10

Step 6. Appliqué the pieces to the block, then make a small slit in the background fabric and use a pair of tweezers to remove the freezer paper.

Method 2: Freezer Paper Appliqué

Follow Steps 1 through 4 under "Method 1: Freezer Paper Appliqué." Leaving the freezer paper adhered to the right side of your fabric, pin the piece to the background fabric. As you stitch the appliqué to the background, turn under the seam allowance on the edge of the freezer paper. Use the edge of the paper as a guide for the fold of your fabric. After your appliqué is stitched in place, gently peel off the freezer paper.

MAKING BIAS VINES

Some of the projects in this book include sashing or borders with appliqué bias strips for vines. The directions specify the size fabric square required for the individual project, as well as the number of strips needed. The strip width given is the width you will need to cut the strips if you are using bias bars. If you are not using bias bars, the instructions here indicate the formula for determining the width to cut the bias strips.

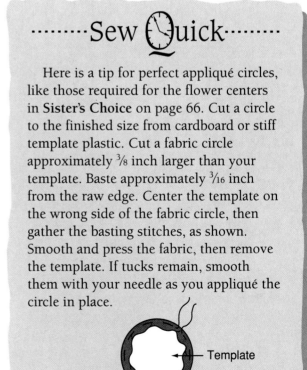

······· Sew Quick·······

Here is a tip for perfect appliqué circles, like those required for the flower centers in **Sister's Choice** on page 66. Cut a circle to the finished size from cardboard or stiff template plastic. Cut a fabric circle approximately ³/₈ inch larger than your template. Baste approximately ³/₁₆ inch from the raw edge. Center the template on the wrong side of the fabric circle, then gather the basting stitches, as shown. Smooth and press the fabric, then remove the template. If tucks remain, smooth them with your needle as you appliqué the circle in place.

← Template

Gather and press

Step 1. Mark and cut a 45 degree angle on the vine fabric, as shown in **Diagram 11A.**

Step 2. Cut bias strips parallel to the first 45 degree cut, as shown in **Diagram 11B.** If you are using the fold method described in Step 3, multiply the desired finished width of the vine by 3, add ¼ inch to that figure, and cut. For example, if you want a vine to finish at ¾ inch wide, the bias strips should measure 2½ inches.

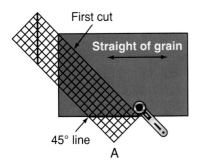

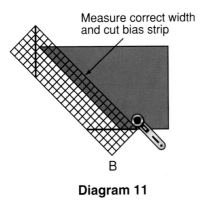

Diagram 11

Step 3. Fold each strip into thirds, as shown in **Diagram 12.** Make sure that the raw edges will be concealed by the folded edges. Press carefully. Position, pin or baste, then appliqué the vines in place, as instructed in the project directions.

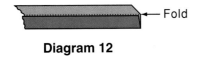

Diagram 12

USING BIAS BARS

Using bias bars is particularly helpful when you need long, narrow stems or vines. Bias bars, which are sold in sets of several widths, are made to withstand the heat of an iron.

Step 1. Cut a bias strip, as shown in **Diagram 11.** The chart below lists cut widths for three sizes of bias strips. **Note: These widths apply only to strips cut for bias bars.**

Finished Width	Cut Width
⅛ inch	⅞ inch
¼ inch	1⅛ inches
⅜ inch	1⅜ inches

Step 2. Fold the strip in half lengthwise, with wrong sides together. Press lightly to hold the edges of the fabric together as you stitch. To avoid stretching, set the iron down to press one section, lift the iron, set it down and press a different section, and repeat until the entire strip has been pressed. Sew the raw edges together, using a ¼-inch seam allowance. Trim the seam allowance to approximately ⅛ inch, as shown in **Diagram 13A.**

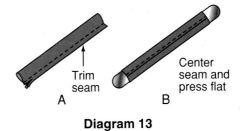

Diagram 13

Step 3. Insert the appropriate-size bias bar into the tube. Turn the tube slightly to center the seam along the flat edge of the bar, as shown in **Diagram 13B.** Dampen the fabric with water or spray starch, and press the seam allowance to one side.

Step 4. Flip the tube over, and check to make sure the seam will be hidden when the strip is appliquéd to the quilt. When you are satisfied with the appearance, press the top side of the tube and remove the bias bar. If the vines are particularly long, you will need to slide the bias bar along the inside of the fabric tube to press the entire length before removing the bar.

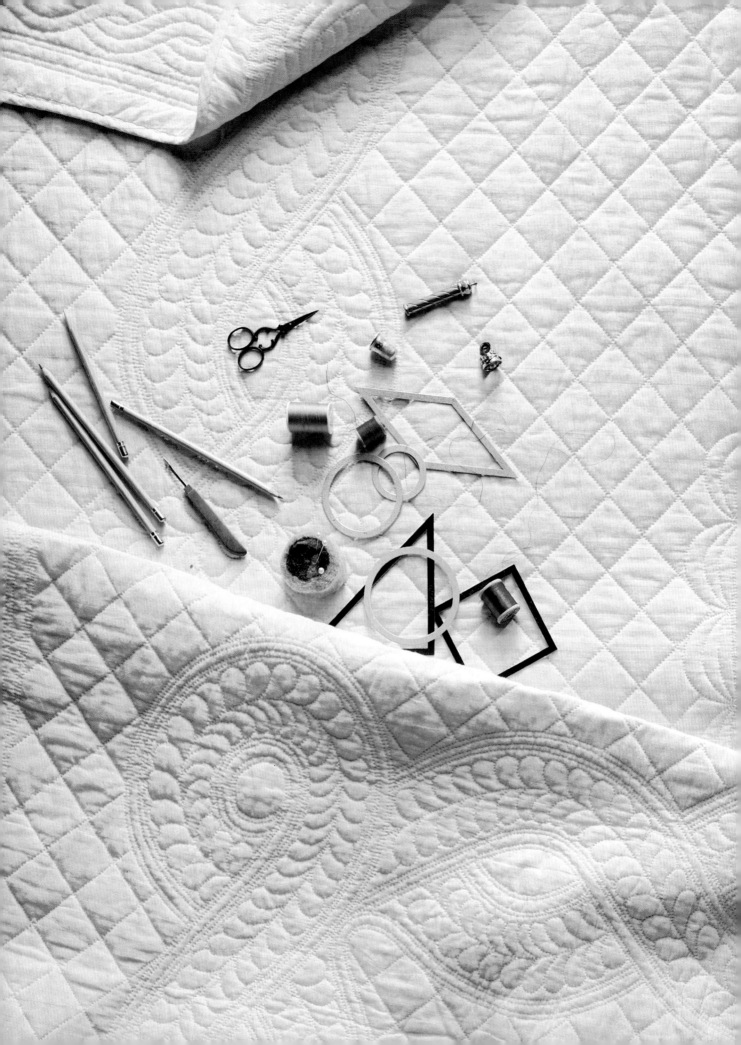

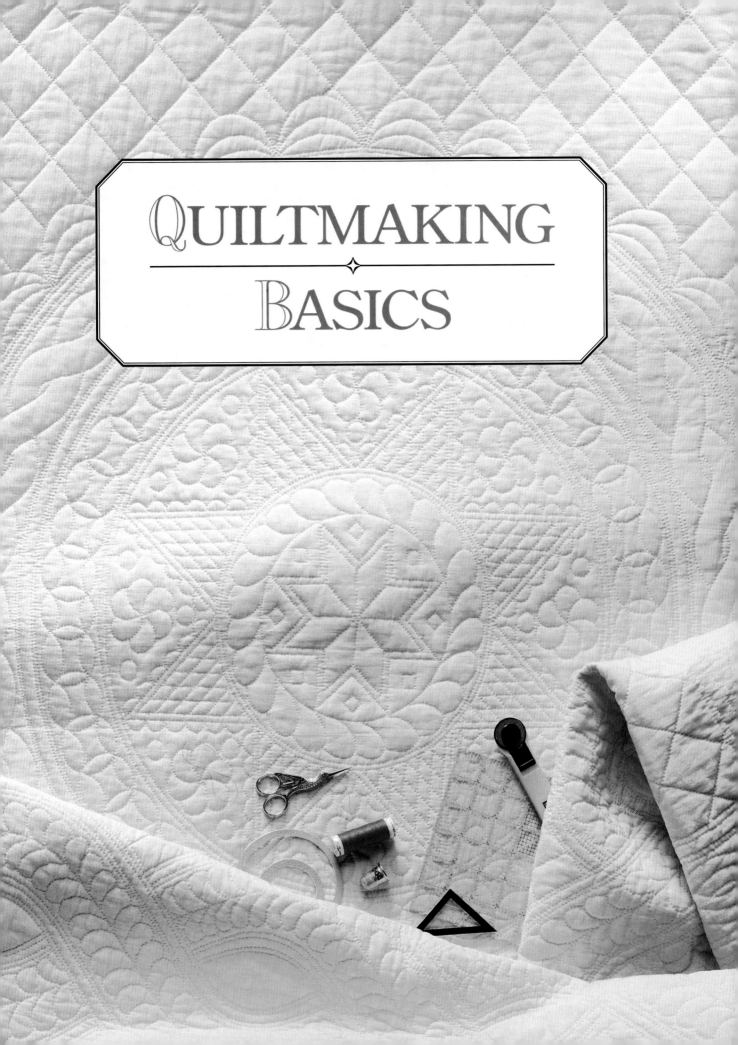

QUILTMAKING
BASICS

This section provides a refresher course in basic quiltmaking techniques. Refer to it as needed; it will help not only with the projects in this book but also with all your quiltmaking.

QUILTMAKER'S BASIC SUPPLY LIST

Here's a list of items you should have on hand before beginning a project.

• **Iron and ironing board:** Make sure these are set up near your sewing machine. Careful pressing leads to accurate piecing.

• **Needles:** The two types of needles commonly used by quilters are *betweens,* short needles used for hand quilting, and *sharps,* long, very thin needles used for appliqué and hand piecing. The thickness of hand-sewing needles decreases as their size designation increases. For instance, a size 12 needle is smaller than a size 10.

• **Rotary cutter, plastic ruler, and cutting mat:** Fabric can be cut quickly and accurately with rotary-cutting equipment. There are a variety of cutters available, all with slightly different handle styles and safety latches. Rigid, see-through acrylic rulers are used with rotary cutters. A 6 × 24-inch ruler is a good size; for the most versatility, be sure it has 45 and 60 degree angle markings. A 14-inch square ruler will also be helpful for making sure blocks are square. Always use a special mat with a rotary cutter. The mat protects the work surface and helps to grip the fabric. Purchase the largest mat practical for your sewing area. A good all-purpose size is 18 × 24 inches.

• **Safety pins:** These are generally used to baste quilts for machine quilting. Use rustproof nickel-plated brass safety pins, preferably in size #0.

• **Scissors:** You'll need several pairs of scissors—shears for cutting fabric, general scissors for cutting paper and template plastic, and small, sharp embroidery scissors for trimming threads.

• **Seam ripper:** A seam ripper with a small, extra-fine blade slips easily under any stitch length.

• **Sewing machine:** Any machine with a straight stitch is suitable for piecing quilt blocks. Follow the manufacturer's recommendations for cleaning and servicing your sewing machine.

• **Straight pins:** Choose long, thin pins with glass or plastic heads that are easy to see against fabric so that you don't forget to remove one.

• **Template material:** Sheets of clear and opaque template plastic can be purchased at most quilt or craft shops. Gridded plastic is also available and may help you to draw shapes more easily. Various weights of cardboard can also be used for templates, including common household items like cereal boxes, posterboard, and manila file folders.

• **Thimbles:** For hand quilting, a thimble is almost essential. Look for one that fits the finger you use to push the needle. The thimble should be snug enough to stay put when you shake your hand. There should be a bit of space between the end of your finger and the inside of the thimble.

• **Thread:** For hand or machine piecing, 100 percent cotton thread is a traditional favorite. Cotton-covered polyester is also acceptable. For hand quilting, use 100 percent cotton quilting thread. For machine quilting, you may want to try clear nylon thread as the top thread, with cotton thread in the bobbin.

• **Tweezers:** Keep a pair of tweezers handy for removing bits of thread from ripped-out seams and for pulling away scraps of removable foundations. Regular cosmetic tweezers will work fine.

SELECTING AND PREPARING FABRICS

The traditional fabric choice for quilts is 100 percent cotton. It handles well, is easy to care for, presses easily, and frays less than synthetic blends.

The yardages in this book are generous estimates based on 44/45-inch-wide fabrics. It's a good idea to always purchase a bit more fabric than necessary to compensate for shrinkage and occasional cutting errors.

Prewash your fabrics using warm water and a mild soap or detergent. Test for colorfastness by first soaking a scrap in warm water. If colors bleed, set the dye by soaking the whole piece of fabric in a solution of 3 parts cold water to 1 part vinegar. Rinse the fabric several times in warm water. If it still bleeds, don't use it in a quilt that will need laundering—save it for a wallhanging that won't get a lot of use.

After washing, preshrink your fabric by drying it in a dryer on the medium setting. To keep wrinkles under control, remove the fabric from the dryer while it's still slightly damp and press it immediately with a hot iron.

CUTTING FABRIC

The cutting instructions for each project follow the list of materials. Whenever possible, the instructions are written to take advantage of quick rotary-cutting techniques. In addition, some projects include patterns for those who prefer to make templates and scissor cut individual pieces.

Although rotary cutting can be faster and more accurate than cutting with scissors, it has one disadvantage: It does not always result in the most efficient use of fabric. In some cases, the method results in long strips of leftover fabric. Don't think of these as waste; just add them to your scrap bag for future projects.

Rotary-Cutting Basics

Follow these two safety rules every time you use a rotary cutter: Always cut *away* from yourself, and always slide the blade guard into place as soon as you stop cutting.

Step 1: You can cut several layers of fabric at a time with a rotary cutter. Fold the fabric with the selvage edges together. You can fold it again if you want, doubling the number of layers to be cut.

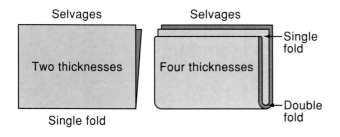

Step 2: To square up the end of the fabric, place a ruled square on the fold and slide a 6 × 24-inch ruler against the side of the square. Hold the ruler in place, remove the square, and cut along the edge of the ruler. If you are left-handed, work from the other end of the fabric.

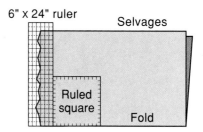

Step 3: For patchwork, cut strips or rectangles on the crosswise grain, then subcut them into smaller pieces as needed. The diagram shows a strip cut into squares.

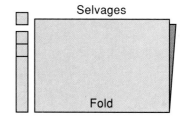

Step 4: A square can be subcut into two triangles by making one diagonal cut (A). Two diagonal cuts yield four triangles (B).

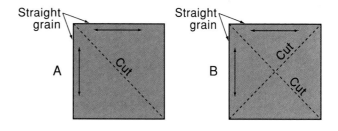

Step 5: Check strips periodically to make sure they're straight and not angled. If they are angled, refold the fabric and square up the edges again.

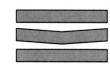

ENLARGING PATTERNS

Every effort has been made to provide full-size pattern pieces. But in some cases, where the pattern piece is too large to fit on the page, only one-half or one-quarter of the pattern is given. Instructions on the pattern piece will tell you where to position the pattern to continue tracing to make a full-size template.

MAKING AND USING TEMPLATES

To make a plastic template, place template plastic over the book page, trace the pattern onto the plastic, and cut out the template. To make a cardboard template, copy the pattern onto tracing paper, glue the paper to the cardboard, and cut out the template. With a permanent marker, record on every template any identification letters and grain lines, as well as the size and name of the block and the number of pieces needed. Always check your templates against the printed pattern for accuracy.

The patchwork patterns in this book are printed with double lines. The inner dashed line is the finished size of the piece, while the outer solid line includes the seam allowance.

For hand piecing: Trace the inner line to make finished-size templates. Cut out the templates on the traced line. Draw around the templates on the wrong side of the fabric, leaving ½ inch between pieces. Then mark ¼-inch seam allowances before you cut out the pieces.

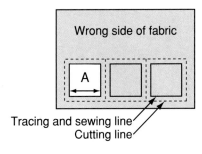

Tracing and sewing line
Cutting line

For machine piecing: Trace the outer solid line on the printed pattern to make templates with seam allowance included. Draw around the templates on the wrong side of the fabric and cut out the pieces on this line.

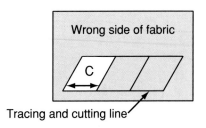

Tracing and cutting line

For appliqué: Appliqué patterns in this book have only a single line and are finished size. Draw around the templates on the right side of the fabric, leaving ½ inch between pieces. Add ⅛- to ¼-inch seam allowances by eye as you cut the pieces.

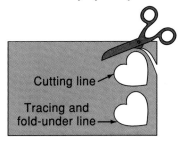

Cutting line →
Tracing and fold-under line →

PIECING BASICS

Standard seam allowance for piecing is ¼ inch. Machine sew a sample seam to test the accuracy of the seam allowance; adjust as needed. For hand piecing, the sewing line is marked on the fabric.

Hand Piecing

Cut fabric pieces using finished-size templates. Place the pieces right sides together, match marked seam lines, and pin. Use a running stitch along the marked line, backstitching every four or five stitches and at the beginning and end of the seam.

When you cross seam allowances of previously joined units, leave the seam allowances free. Backstitch just before you cross, slip the needle through the seam allowance, backstitch just after you cross, then resume stitching the seam.

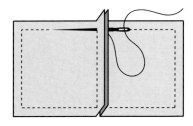

Machine Piecing

Cut the fabric pieces using templates with seam allowances included or using a rotary cutter and ruler without templates. Set the stitch length at 10 to 12 stitches per inch.

Place the fabric pieces right sides together, then sew from raw edge to raw edge. Press seams before crossing them with other seams, pressing toward the darker fabric whenever possible.

Chain piecing: Use this technique when you need to sew more than one of the same type of unit. Place the fabric pieces right sides together and, without lifting the presser foot or cutting the thread, run the pairs through the sewing machine one after another. Once all the units you need have been sewn, snip them apart and press.

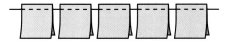

Setting In Pieces

Pattern pieces must sometimes be set into angles created by other pieces, as shown in the diagram. Here, pieces A, B, and C are set into the angles created by the four joined diamond pieces.

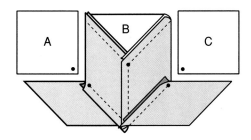

Step 1: Keep the seam allowances open where the piece is to be set in. Begin by sewing the first seam in the usual manner, beginning and ending the seam ¼ inch from the edge of the fabric and backstitching at each end.

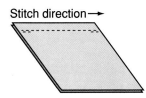

Step 2: Open up the pattern pieces and place the piece to be set in right sides together with one of the first two pieces. Begin the seam ¼ inch from the edge of the fabric and sew to the exact point where the first seam ended, backstitching at the beginning and end of the seam.

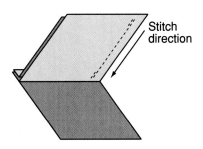

Step 3: Rotate the pattern pieces so that you are ready to sew the final seam. Keeping the seam allowances free, sew from the point where the last seam ended to ¼ inch from the edge of the piece.

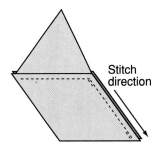

Step 4: Press the seams so that as many of them as possible lie flat. The finished unit should look like the one shown here.

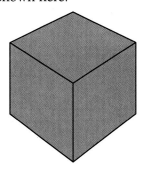

APPLIQUÉ BASICS

Review "Making and Using Templates" to learn how to prepare templates for appliqué. Lightly draw around each template on the right side of the fabric using a pencil or other nonpermanent marker. These are the fold-under lines. Cut out the pieces ⅛ to ¼ inch to the outside of the marked lines.

The Needle-Turn Method

Pin the pieces in position on the background fabric, always working in order from the background to the foreground. For best results, don't turn under or appliqué edges that will be covered by other appliqué pieces. Use a thread color that matches the fabric of the appliqué piece.

Step 1: Bring the needle up from under the appliqué patch exactly on the drawn line. Fold under the seam allowance on the line to neatly encase the knot.

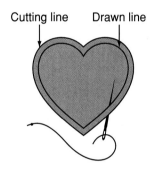

Cutting line   Drawn line

Step 2: Insert the tip of the needle into the background fabric right next to where the thread comes out of the appliqué piece. Bring the needle out of the background fabric approximately ¹⁄₁₆ inch away from and up through the very edge of the fold, completing the first stitch.

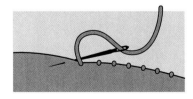

Step 3: Repeat this process for each stitch, using the tip and shank of your appliqué needle to turn under ½-inch-long sections of seam allowance at a time. As you turn under a section, press it flat with your thumb and then stitch it in place, as shown.

PRESSING BASICS

Proper pressing can make a big difference in the appearance of a finished block or quilt top. It allows patchwork to open up to its full size, permits more precise matching of seams, and results in smooth, flat work. Quilters are divided on the issue of whether a steam or dry iron is best; experiment to see which works best for you. Keep these tips in mind:

• Press seam allowances to one side, not open. Whenever possible, press toward the darker fabric. If you find you must press toward a lighter fabric, trim the dark seam allowance slightly to prevent show-through.

• Press seams of adjacent rows of blocks, or rows within blocks, in opposite directions. The pressed seams will fit together snugly, producing precise intersections.

• Press, don't iron. Bring the iron down gently and firmly. This is especially important if you are using steam.

• To press appliqués, lay a towel on the ironing board, turn the piece right side down on the towel, and press very gently on the back side.

ASSEMBLING QUILT TOPS

Lay out all the blocks for your quilt top using the quilt diagram or photo as a guide to placement. Pin and sew the blocks together in vertical or horizontal rows for straight-set quilts and in diagonal rows for diagonal-set quilts. Press the seam allowances in opposite directions from row to row so that the seams will fit together snugly when rows are joined.

To keep a large quilt top manageable, join rows into pairs first and then join the pairs. When pressing a completed quilt top, press on the back side first, carefully clipping and removing hanging threads; then press the front.

MITERING BORDERS

Step 1: Start by measuring the length of your finished quilt top through the center. Add to that figure two times the width of the border, plus 5 inches extra. This is the length you need to cut the two side borders. For example, if the quilt top is 48 inches long and the border is 4 inches wide, you need two borders that are each 61 inches long (48 + 4 + 4 + 5 = 61). In the same manner, calculate the length of the top and bottom borders, then cut the borders.

Step 2: Sew each of the borders to the quilt top, beginning and ending the seams ¼ inch from the edge of the quilt. Press the border seams flat from the right side of the quilt.

Step 3: Working at one corner of the quilt, place one border on top of the adjacent border. Fold the top border under so that it meets the edge of the other border and forms a 45 degree angle, as shown in the diagram. If you are working with a plaid or striped border, check to make sure the stripes match along this folded edge. Press the fold in place.

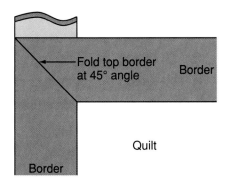

Step 4: Fold the quilt top with right sides together and align the edges of the borders. With the pressed fold as the corner seam line and the

body of the quilt out of the way, sew from the inner corner to the outer corner, as shown in the diagram.

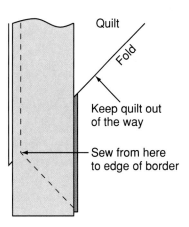

Step 5: Unfold the quilt and check to make sure that all points match and the miter is flat. Trim the border seam allowance to ¼ inch and press the seam open.

Step 6: Repeat Steps 3 through 5 for the three remaining corners.

MARKING QUILTING DESIGNS

To mark a quilting design, use a commercially made stencil, make your own stencil using a sheet of plastic, or trace the design from a book page. Use a nonpermanent marker, such as a silver or white pencil, chalk pencil, or chalk marker, that will be visible on the fabric. You can even mark with a 0.5 mm lead pencil, but be sure to mark lightly.

If you are using a quilt design from a book, either trace the design onto tracing paper or photocopy it. If the pattern will be used many times, glue it to cardboard to make it sturdy.

For light-color fabrics that you can see through, place the pattern under the quilt top and trace the quilting design directly onto the fabric. Mark in a thin, continuous line that will be covered by the quilting thread.

With dark fabrics, mark from the top by drawing around a hard-edged design template. To make a simple template, trace the design onto template plastic and cut it out around the outer edge. Trace around the template onto the fabric, then add inner lines by eye.

LAYERING AND BASTING

Carefully preparing the quilt top, batting, and backing will ensure that the finished quilt will lie flat and smooth. Place the backing wrong side up on a large table or clean floor. Center the batting on the backing and smooth out any wrinkles. Center the quilt top right side up on the batting; smooth it out and remove any loose threads.

If you plan to hand quilt, baste the quilt with thread. Use a long darning needle and white thread. Baste outward from the center of the quilt in a grid of horizontal and vertical rows approximately 4 inches apart.

If you plan to machine quilt, baste with safety pins. Thread basting does not hold the layers securely enough during machine quilting, plus the thread is more difficult to remove when quilting is completed. Use rustproof nickel-plated brass safety pins in size #0, starting in the center of the quilt and pinning approximately every 3 inches.

HAND QUILTING

For best results, use a hoop or a frame to hold the quilt layers taut and smooth during quilting. Work with one hand on top of the quilt and the other hand underneath, guiding the needle. Don't worry about the size of your stitches in the beginning; concentrate on making them even, and they will get smaller over time.

Getting started: Thread a needle with quilting thread and knot the end. Insert the needle through the quilt top and batting about 1 inch away from where you will begin stitching. Bring the needle to the surface in position to make the first stitch. Gently tug on the thread to pop the knot through the quilt top and bury it in the batting.

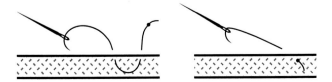

Taking the stitches: Insert the needle through the three layers of the quilt. When you feel the tip of the needle with your underneath finger, gently guide it back up through the quilt. When the needle comes through the top of the quilt, press your thimble on the end with the eye to guide it down again through the quilt layers. Continue to quilt in this manner, taking two or three small running stitches at a time.

Ending a line of stitching: Bring the needle to the top of the quilt just past the last stitch. Make a knot at the surface by bringing the needle under the thread where it comes out of the fabric and up through the loop of thread it creates. Repeat this knot and insert the needle into the hole where the thread comes out of the fabric. Run the needle inside the batting for an inch and bring it back to the surface. Tug gently on the thread to pop the knot into the batting layer. Clip the thread.

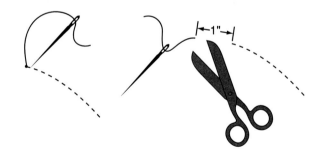

MACHINE QUILTING

For best results when doing machine-guided quilting, use a walking foot (also called an even feed foot) on your sewing machine. For free-motion quilting, use a darning or machine-embroidery foot.

Use thread to match the fabric colors, or use clear nylon thread in the top of the machine and a white or colored thread in the bobbin. To secure the thread at the beginning of a line of stitches, adjust the stitch length on your machine to make several very short stitches, then gradually increase to the regular stitch length. As you near the end of the line, gradually reduce the stitch length so that the last few stitches are very short.

For machine-guided quilting, keep the feed dogs up and move all three layers as smoothly as you can under the needle. To turn a corner in a quilting design, stop with the needle inserted in the fabric, raise the foot, pivot the quilt, lower the foot, and continue stitching.

For free-motion quilting, disengage the feed dogs so you can manipulate the quilt freely as you stitch. Guide the quilt under the needle with both hands, coordinating the speed of the needle with the movement of the quilt to create stitches of consistent length.

MAKING AND ATTACHING BINDING

Double-fold binding, which is also called French-fold binding, can be made from either straight-grain or bias strips. To make double-fold binding, cut strips of fabric four times the finished width of the binding, plus seam allowance. In general, cut strips 2 inches wide for quilts with thin batting or scalloped edges and $2\frac{1}{4}$ to $2\frac{1}{2}$ inches wide for quilts with thicker batting.

Straight-Grain Binding

To make straight-grain binding, cut crosswise strips from the binding fabric in the desired width. Sew them together end to end with diagonal seams.

Place the strips with right sides together so that each strip is set in $\frac{1}{4}$ inch from the end of the other strip. Sew a diagonal seam and trim the excess fabric, leaving a $\frac{1}{4}$-inch seam allowance.

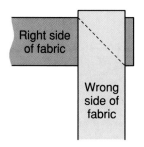

Continuous Bias Binding

Bias binding can be cut in one long strip from a square of fabric that has been cut apart and resewn into a tube. To estimate the number of inches of binding a particular square will produce, use this formula:

Multiply the length of one side by the length of another side, and divide the result by the width of binding you want. Using a 30-inch square and $2\frac{1}{4}$-inch binding as an example: $30 \times 30 = 900$; $900 \div 2\frac{1}{4} = 400$ inches of binding.

Step 1: To make bias binding, cut a square in half diagonally to get two triangles. Place the two triangles right sides together, as shown, and sew with a $\frac{1}{4}$-inch seam. Open out the two pieces and press the seam open.

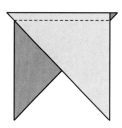

Step 2: Using a pencil and a see-through ruler, mark cutting lines on the wrong side of the fabric in the desired binding width. Draw the lines parallel to the bias edges.

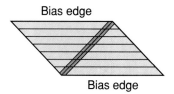

Step 3: Fold the fabric with right sides together, bringing the two nonbias edges together and offsetting them by one strip width (as shown in the diagram at the top of page 122). Pin the edges together, creating a tube, and sew with a $\frac{1}{4}$-inch seam. Press the seam open.

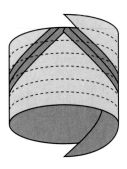

Step 4: Cut on the marked lines, turning the tube to cut one long bias strip.

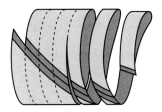

Attaching the Binding

Trim excess batting and backing even with the quilt top. For double-fold binding, fold the long binding strip in half lengthwise, with wrong sides together, and press. Beginning in the middle of a side, not in a corner, place the strip right sides together with the quilt top, align raw edges, and pin.

Step 1: Fold over approximately 1 inch at the beginning of the strip and begin stitching ½ inch from the fold. Sew the binding to the quilt, using a ¼-inch seam and stitching through all layers.

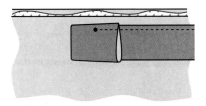

Step 2: As you approach a corner, stop stitching ¼ inch from the raw edge of the corner. Backstitch and remove the quilt from the machine. Fold the binding strip up at a 45 degree angle, as shown in the following diagram on the left. Fold the strip back down so there is a fold at the upper

edge, as shown on the right. Begin sewing ¼ inch from the top edge of the quilt, continuing to the next corner. Miter all four corners in this manner.

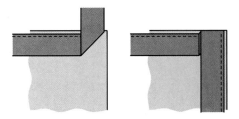

Step 3: To finish the binding seam, overlap the folded-back beginning section with the ending section. Stitch across the fold, allowing the end to extend approximately ½ inch beyond the beginning.

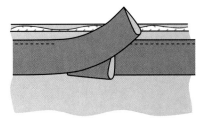

Step 4: Turn the binding to the back of the quilt and blindstitch the folded edge in place, covering the machine stitches with the folded edge. Fold in the adjacent sides on the back and take several stitches in the miter. In the same way, add several stitches to the miters on the front.

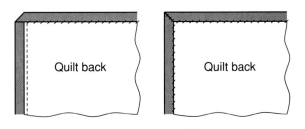

SIGNING YOUR QUILT

Be sure to sign and date your finished quilt. Your finishing touch can be a simple signature in permanent ink or an elaborate inked or embroidered label. Add any other pertinent details that can help family members or quilt collectors 100 years from now understand what went into your labor of love.